I0502825

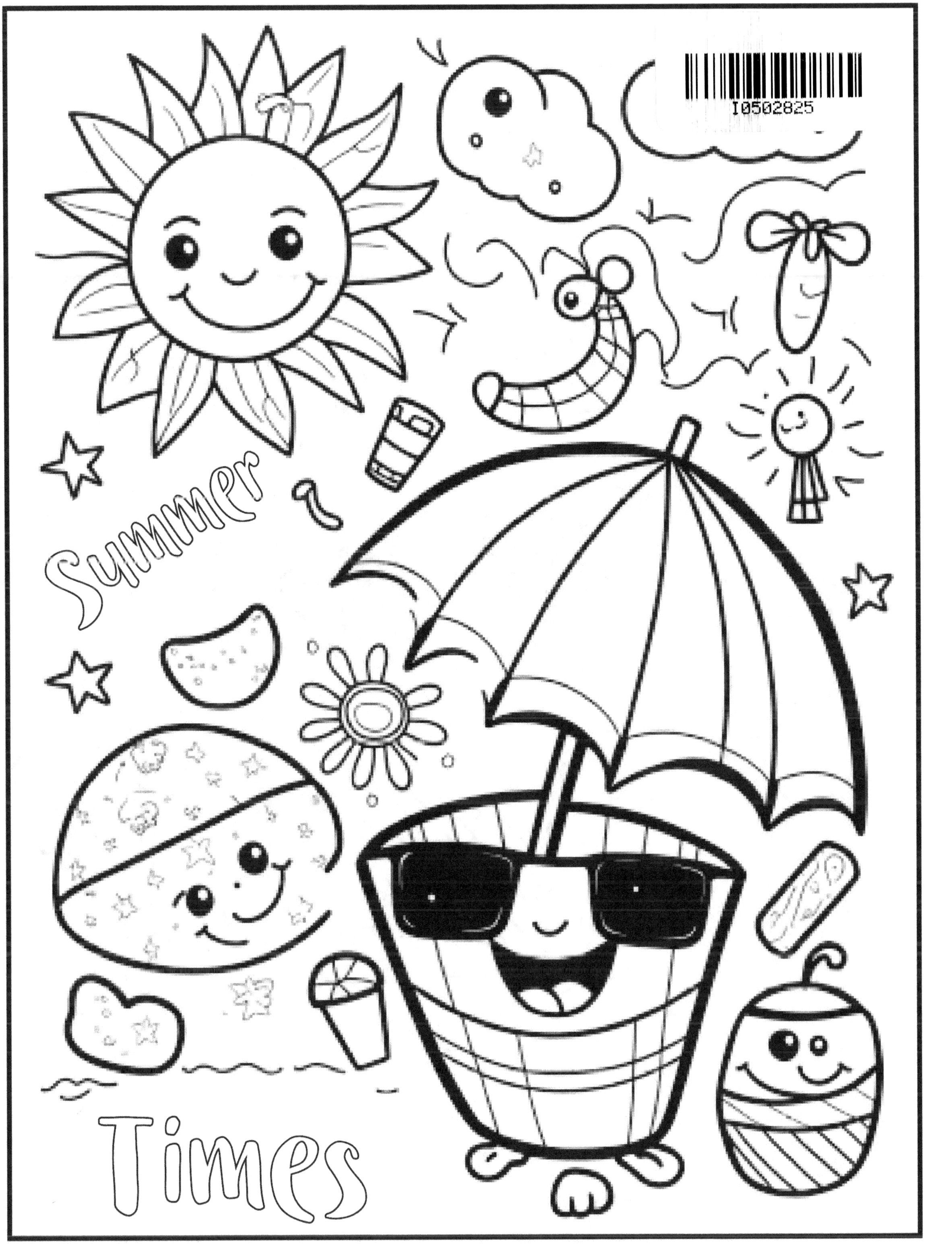

Summer Day

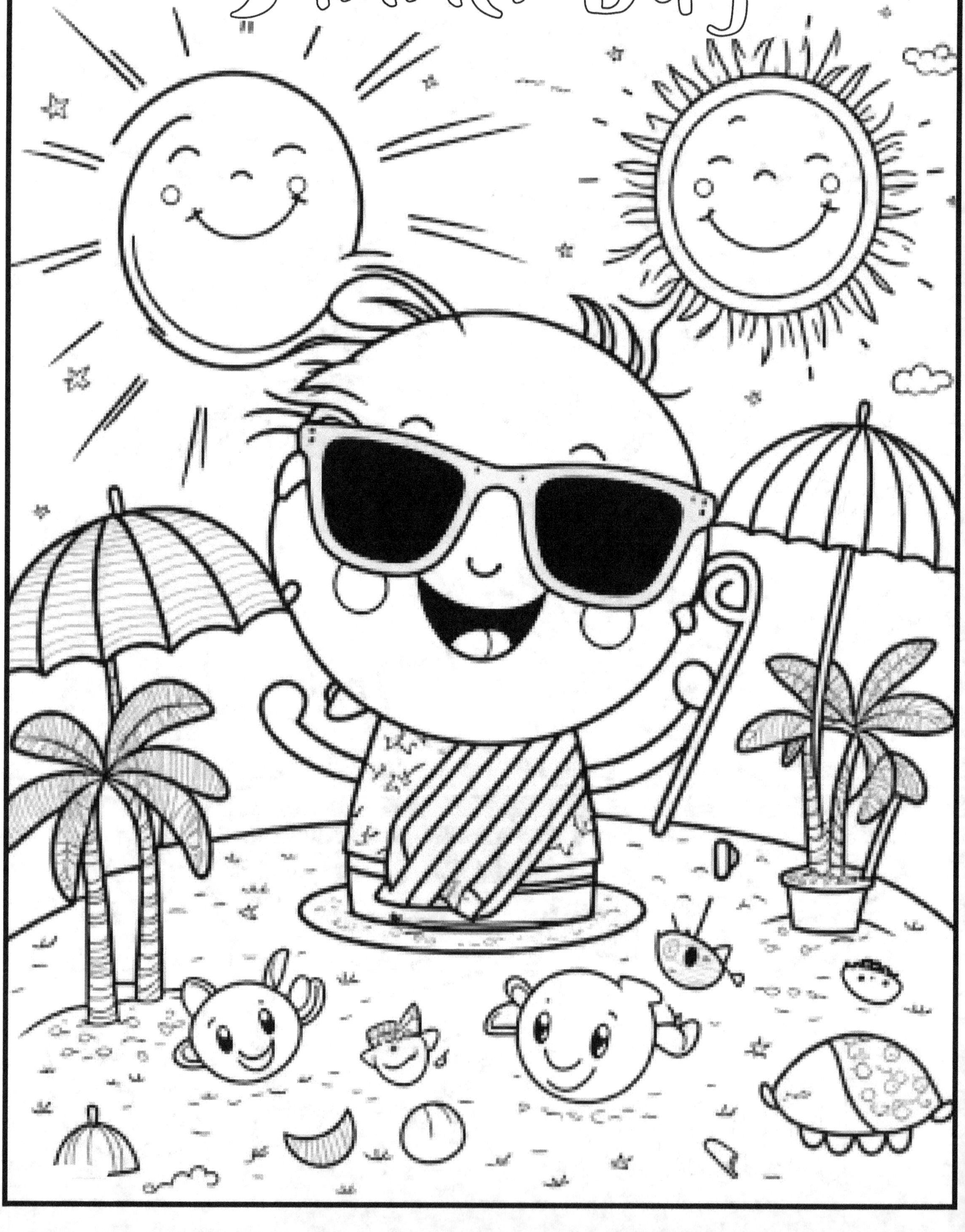

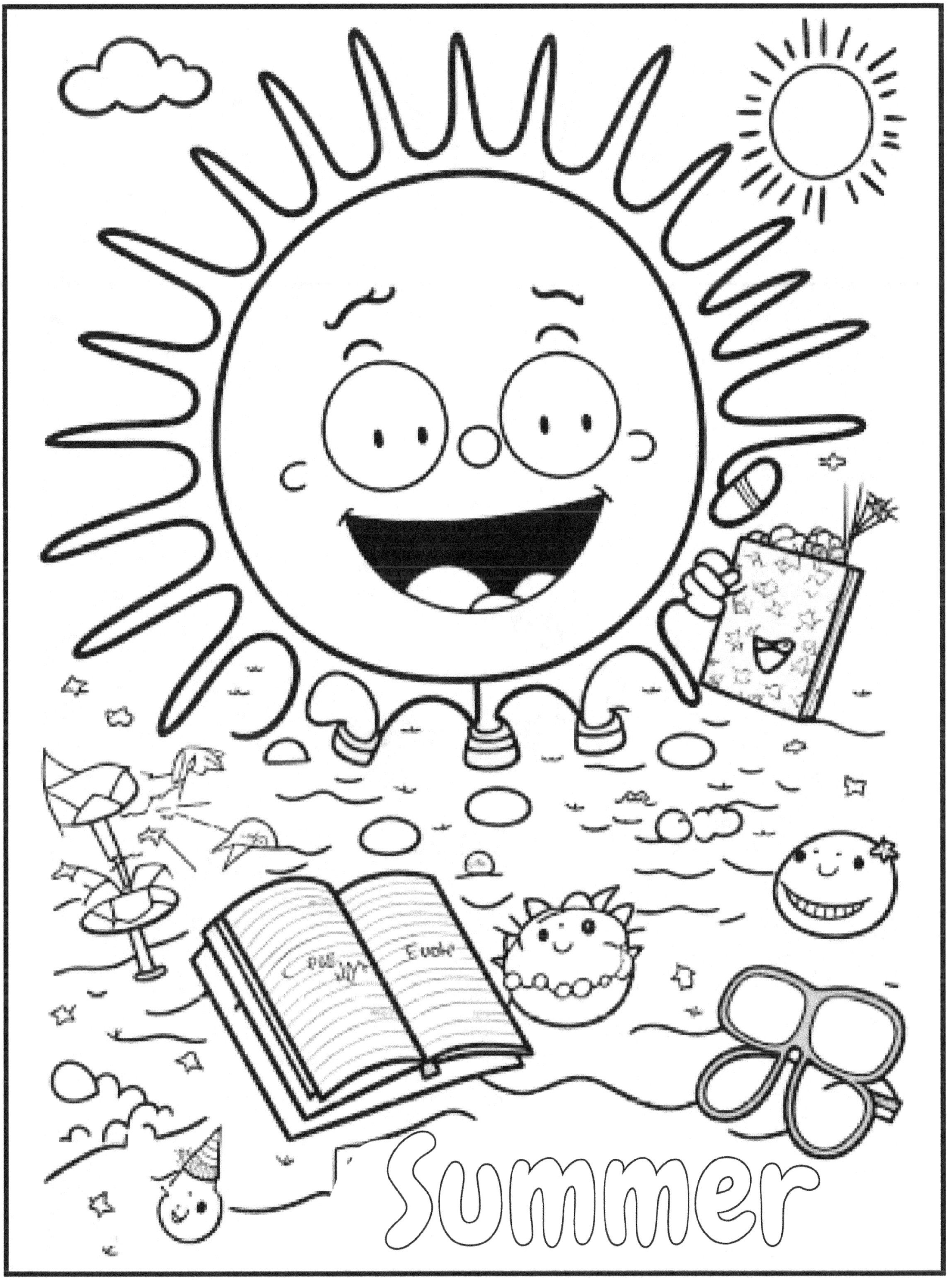
Summer

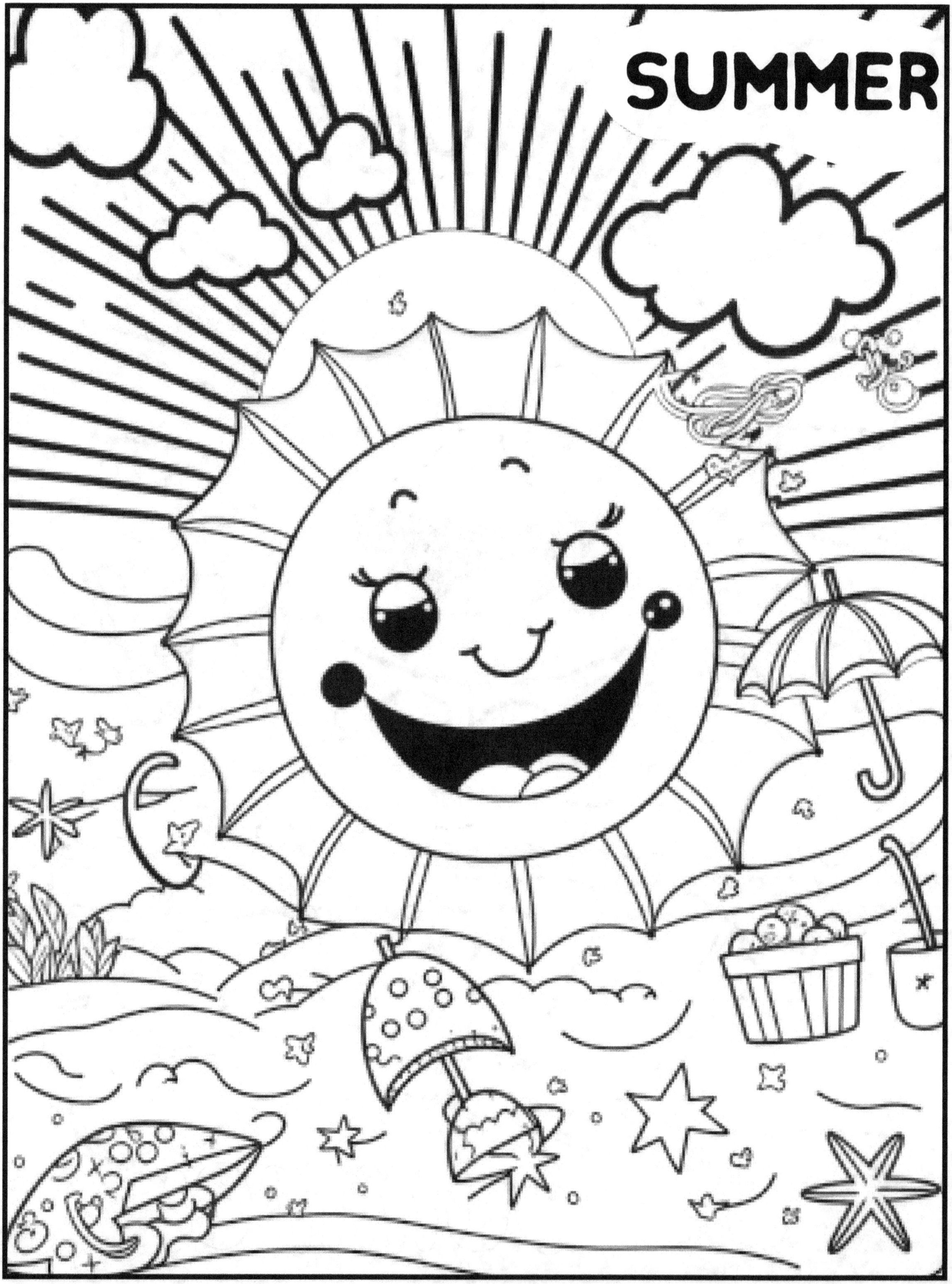
SUMMER

Summer Times

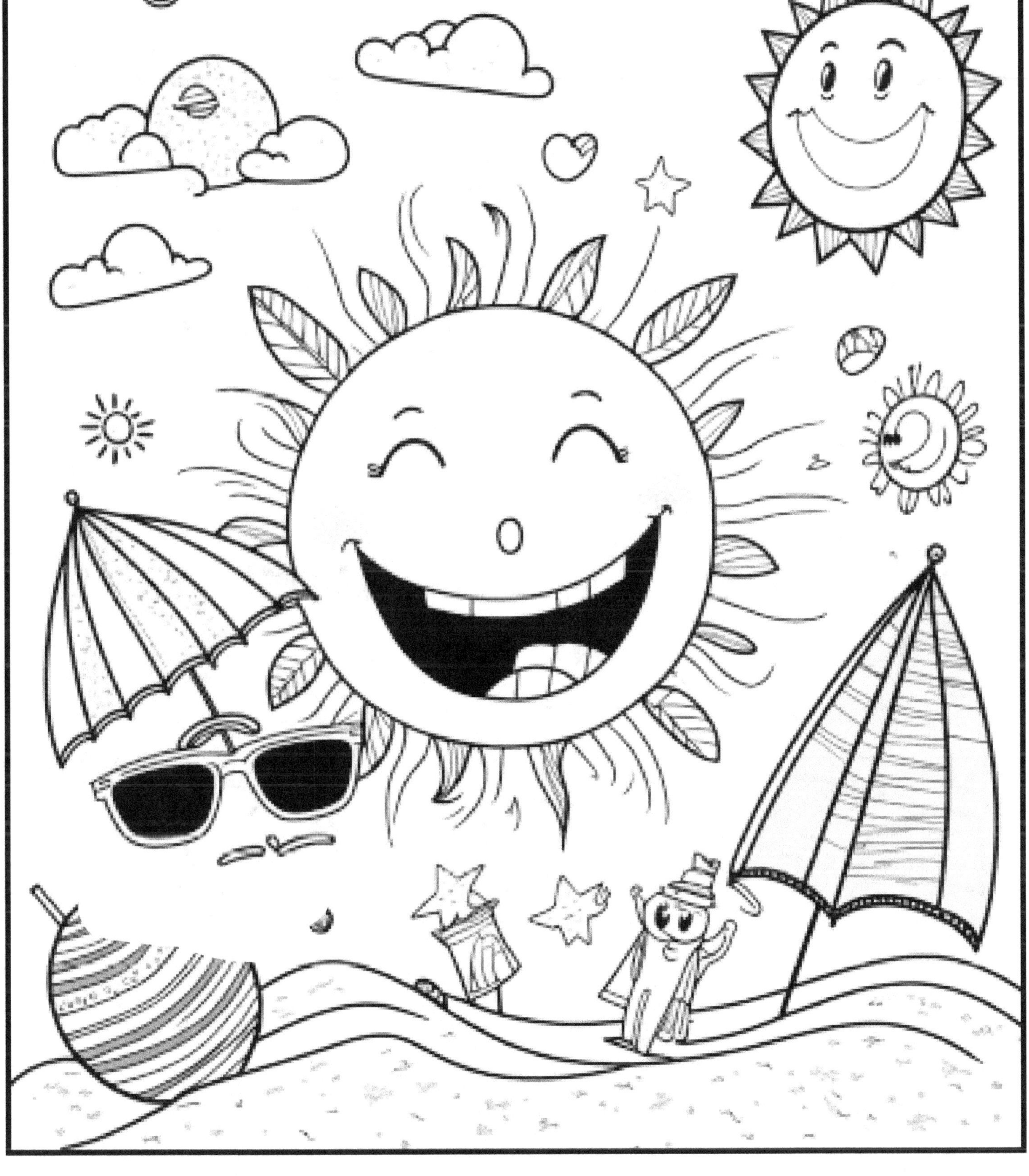

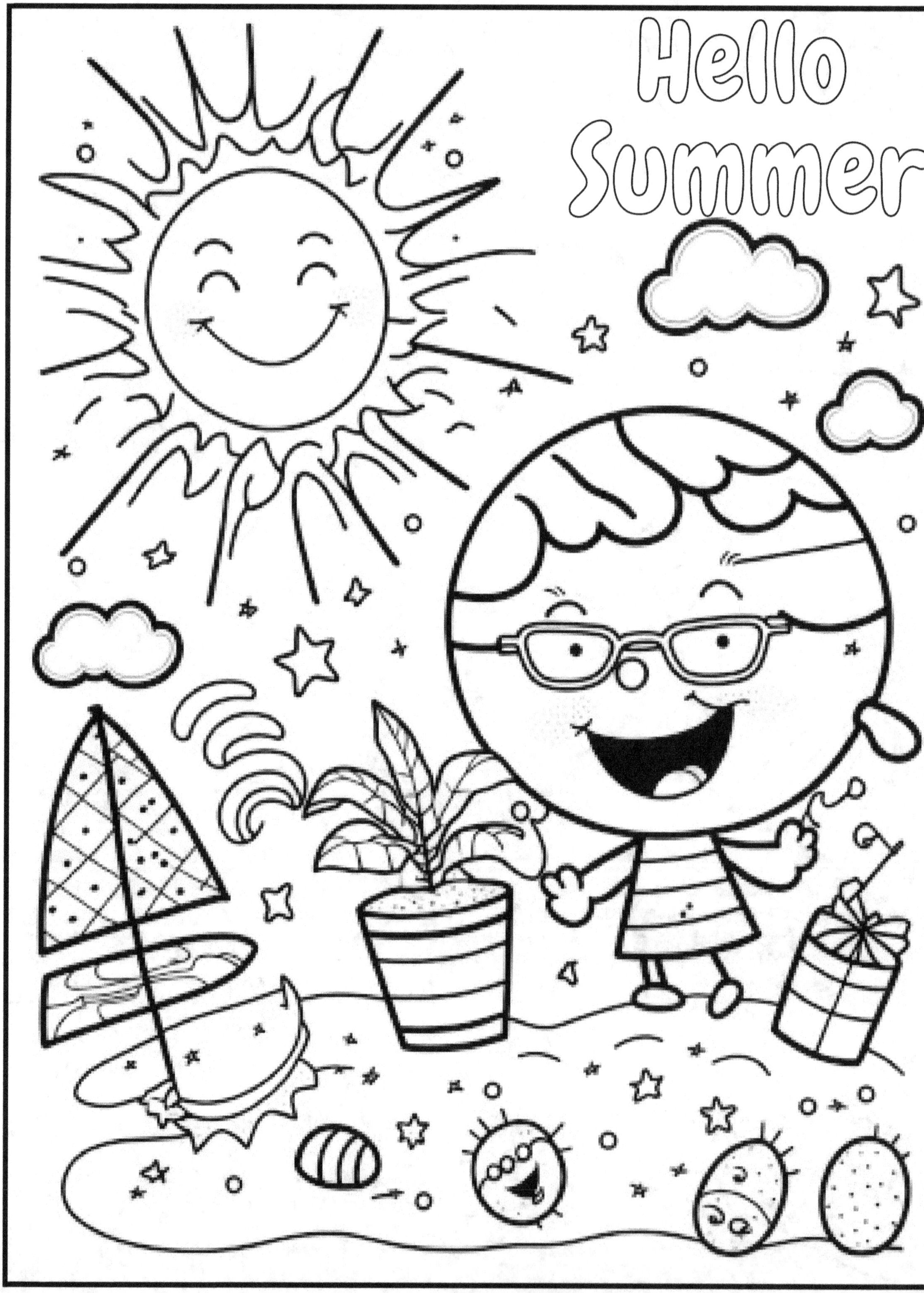
Hello
Summer

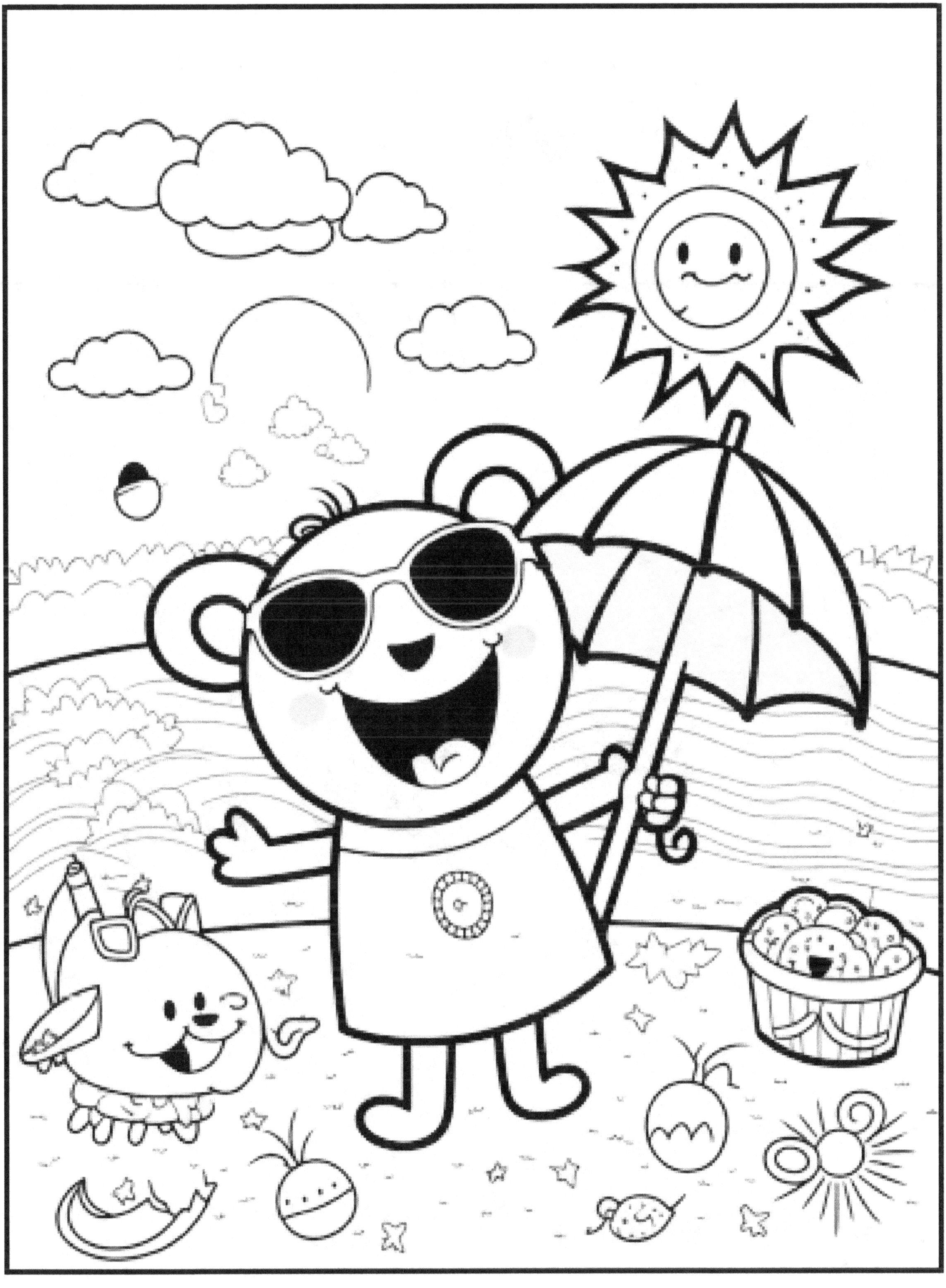

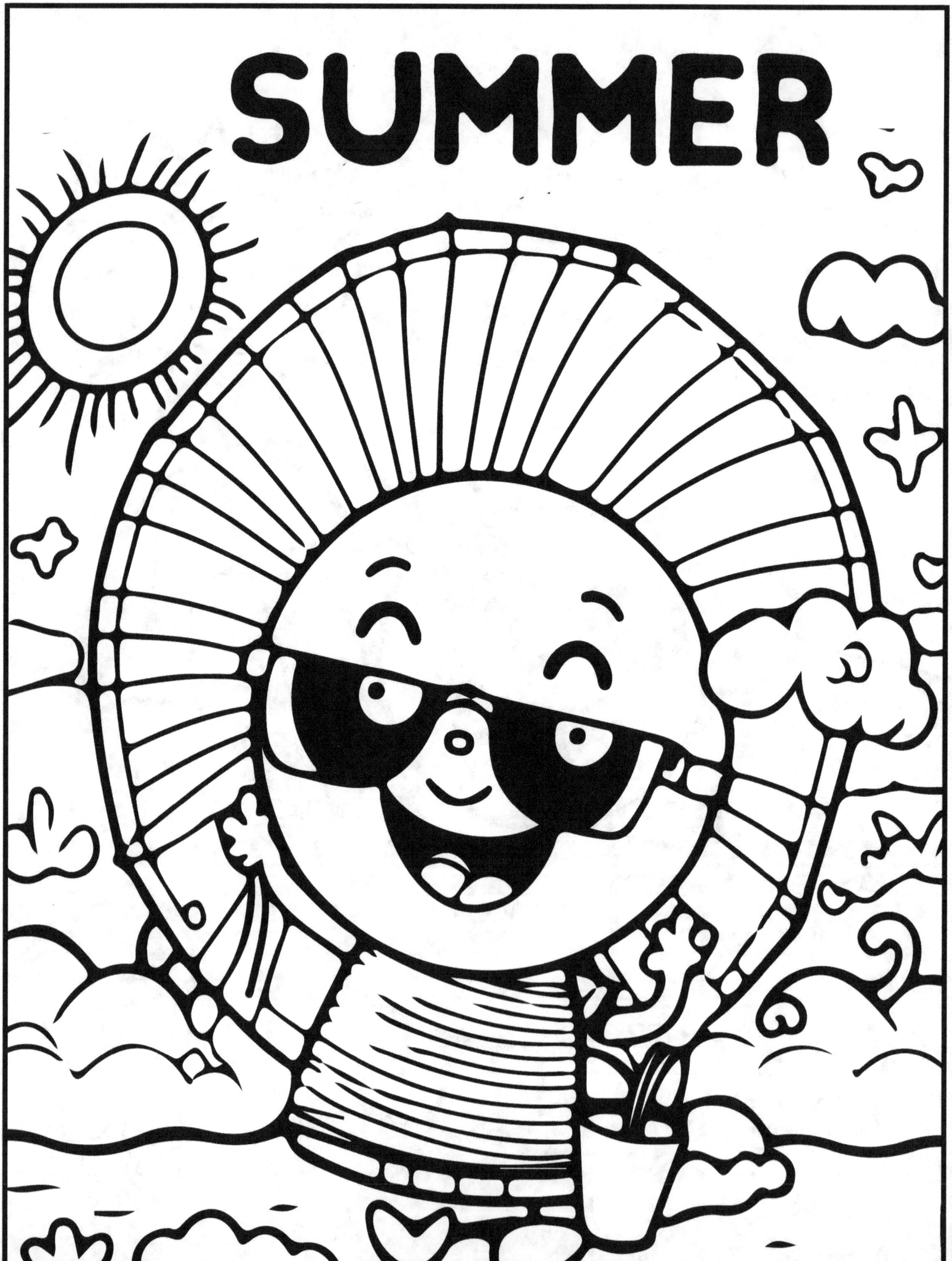
SUMMER

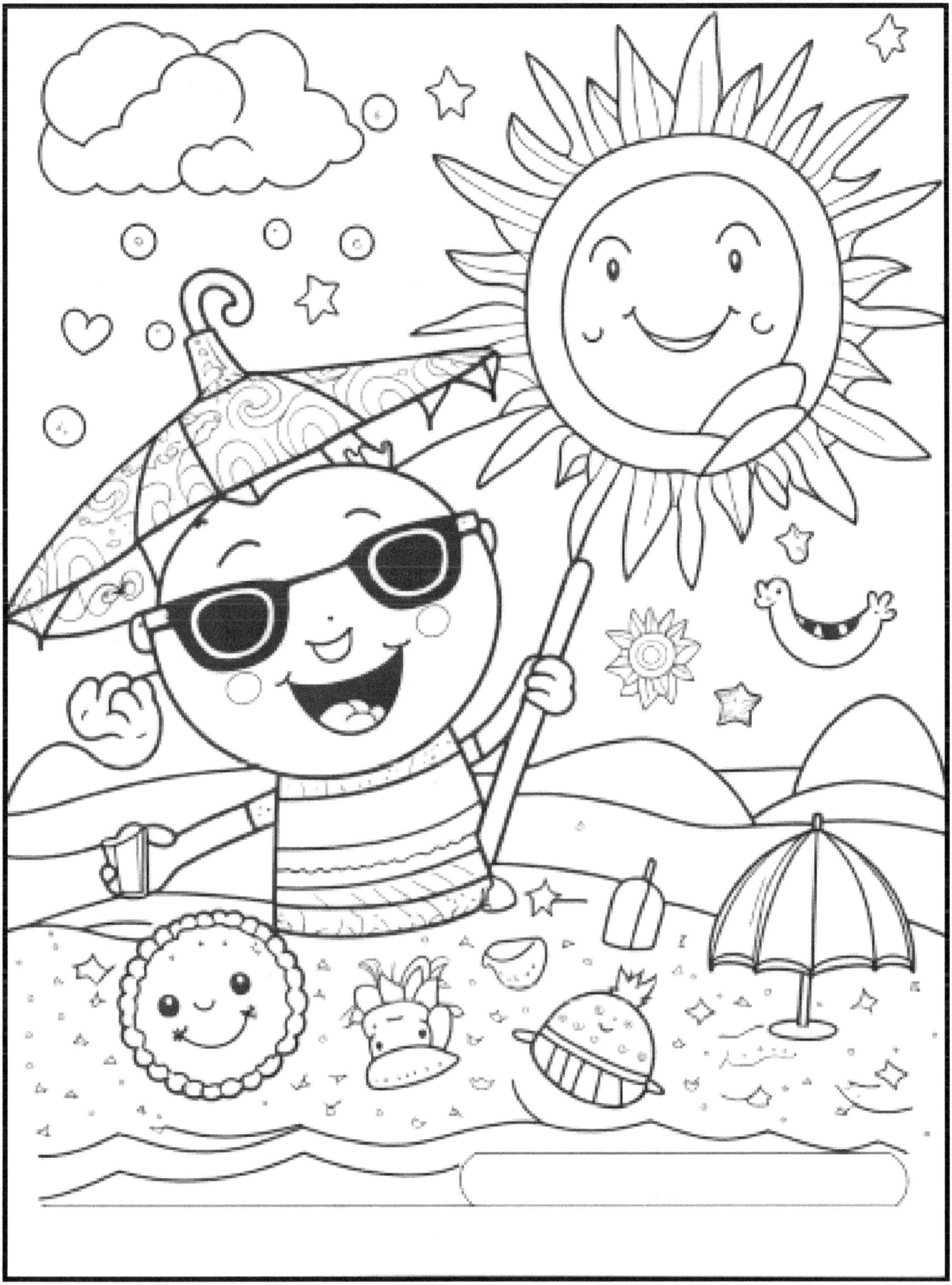

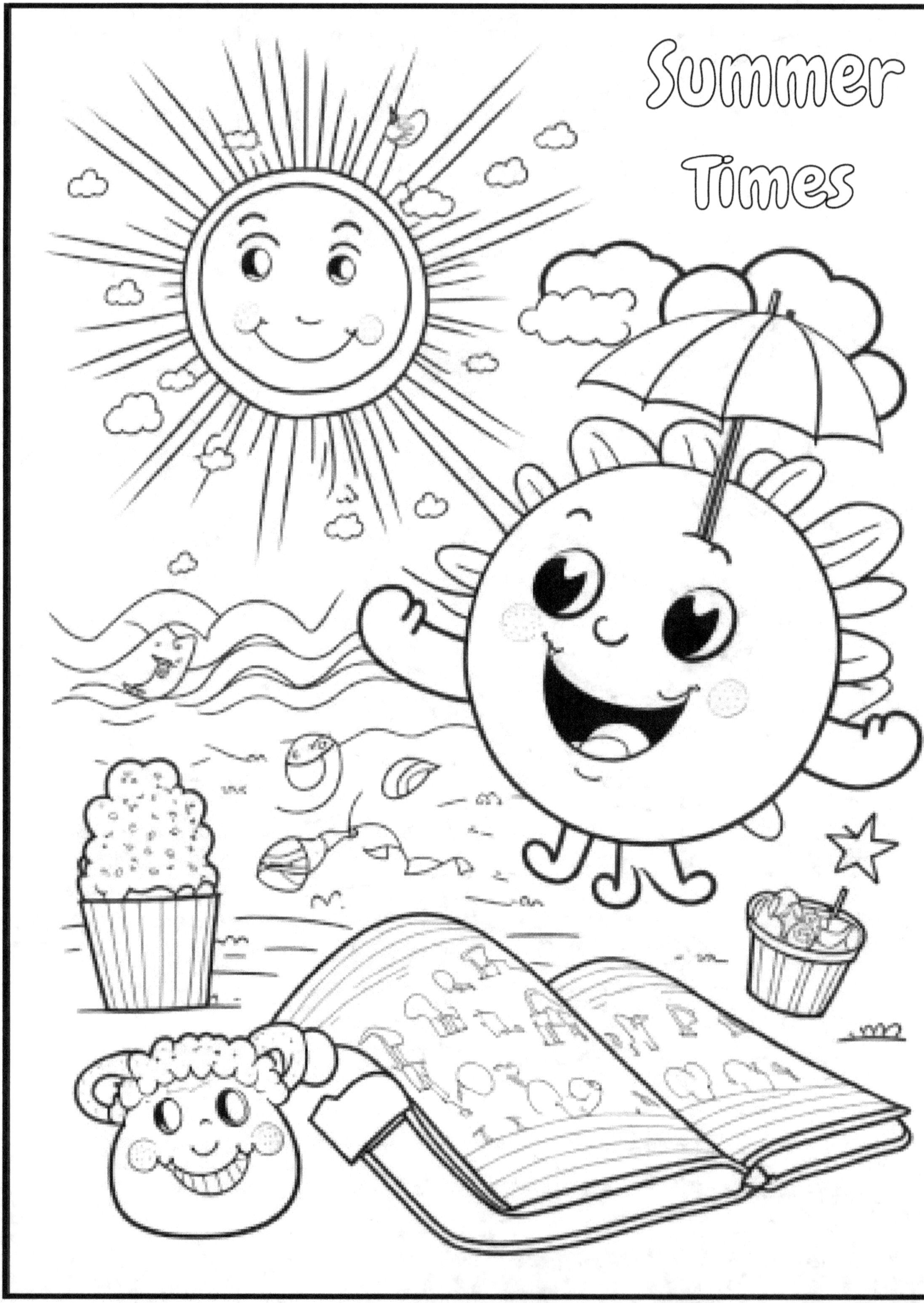
Summer
Times

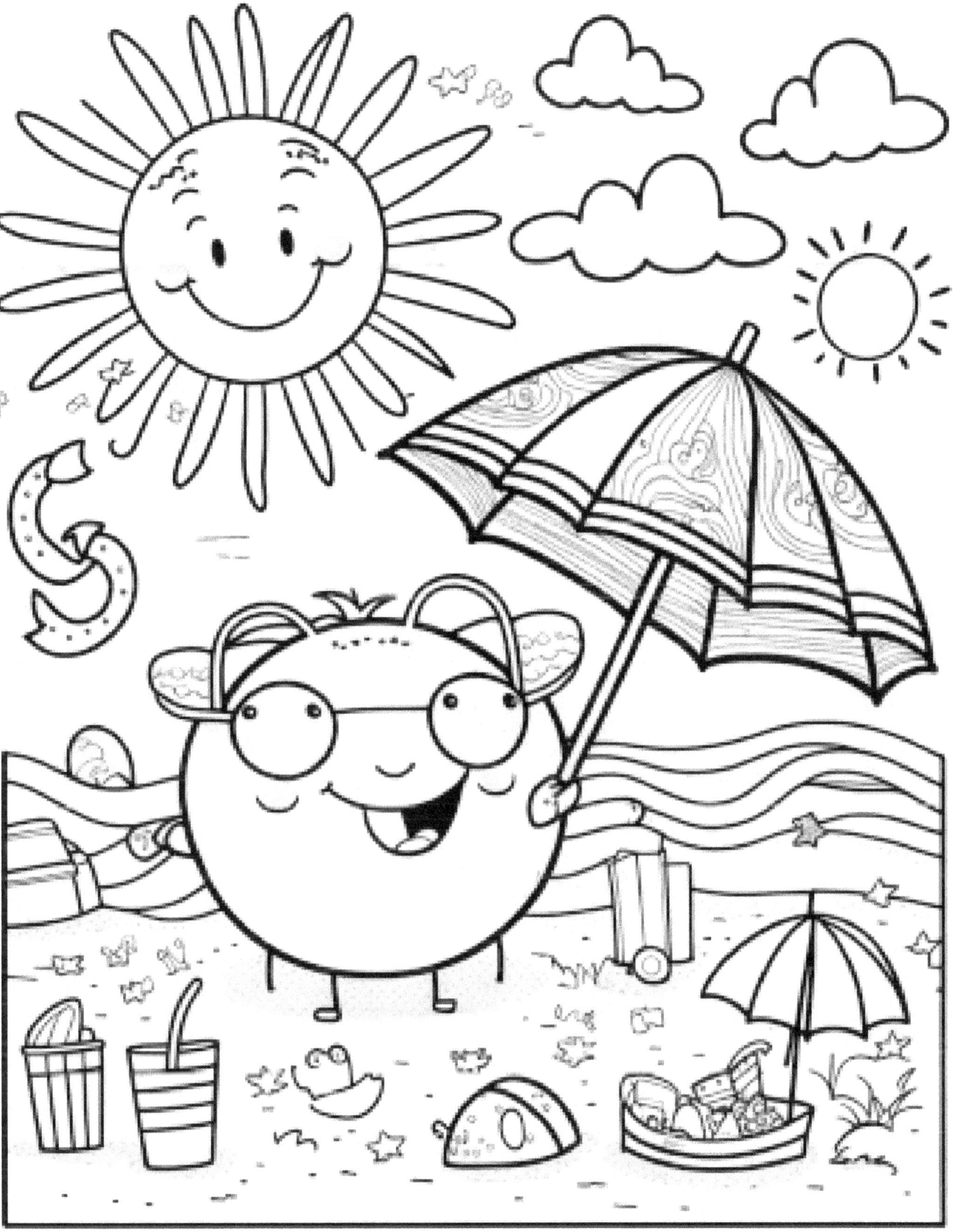

Summer Times

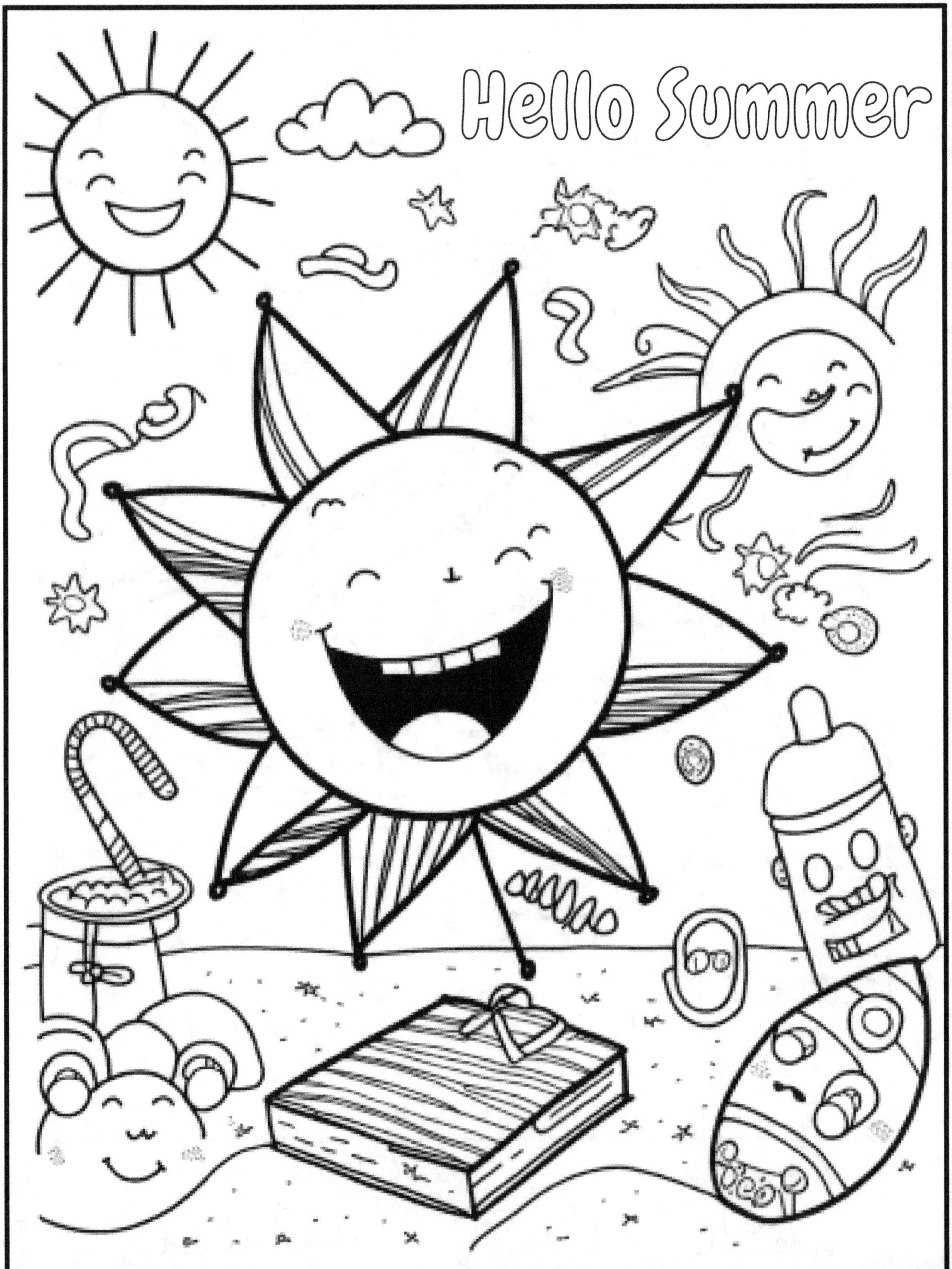
Hello Summer

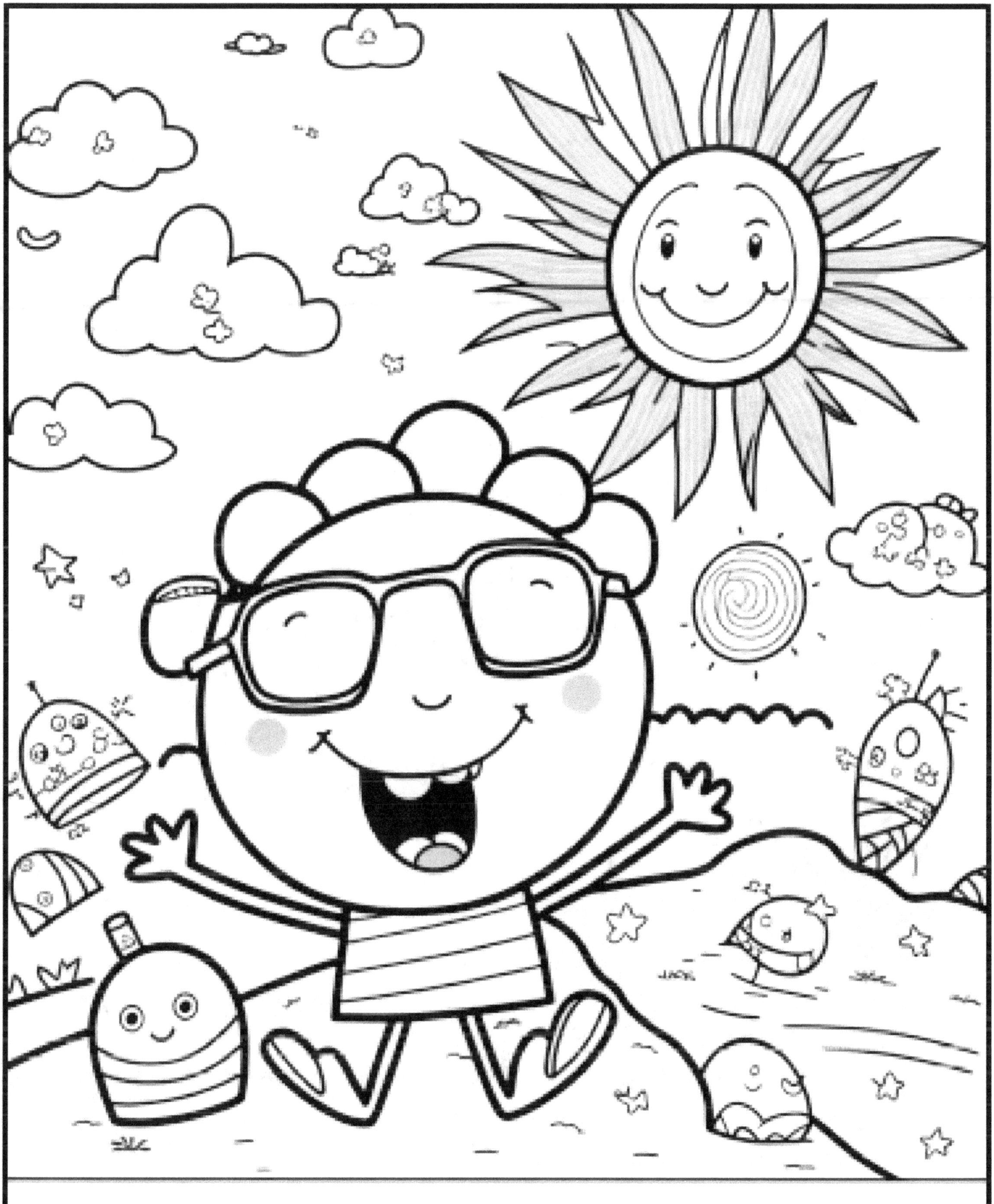

It,s Summer Times

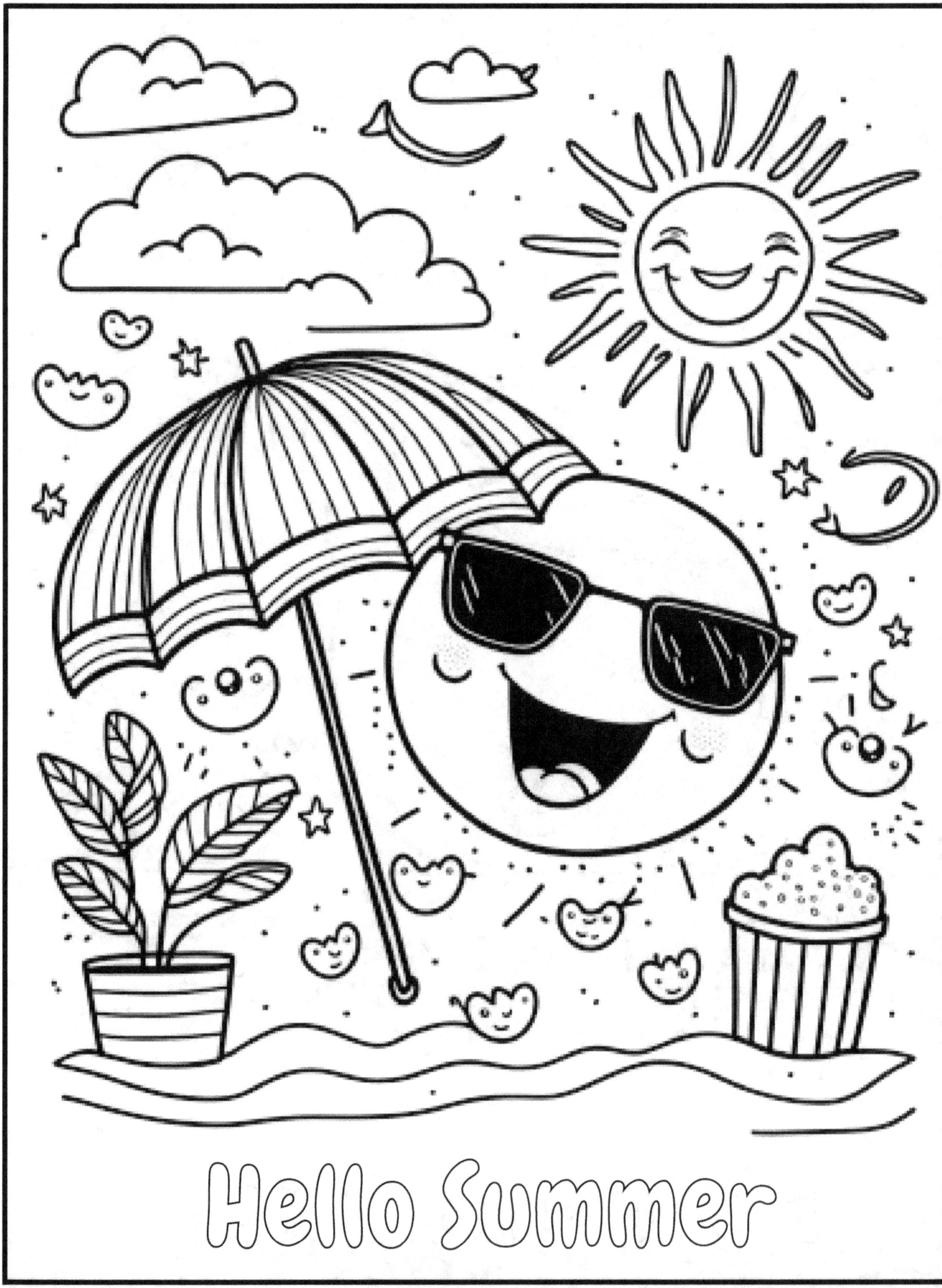
Hello Summer

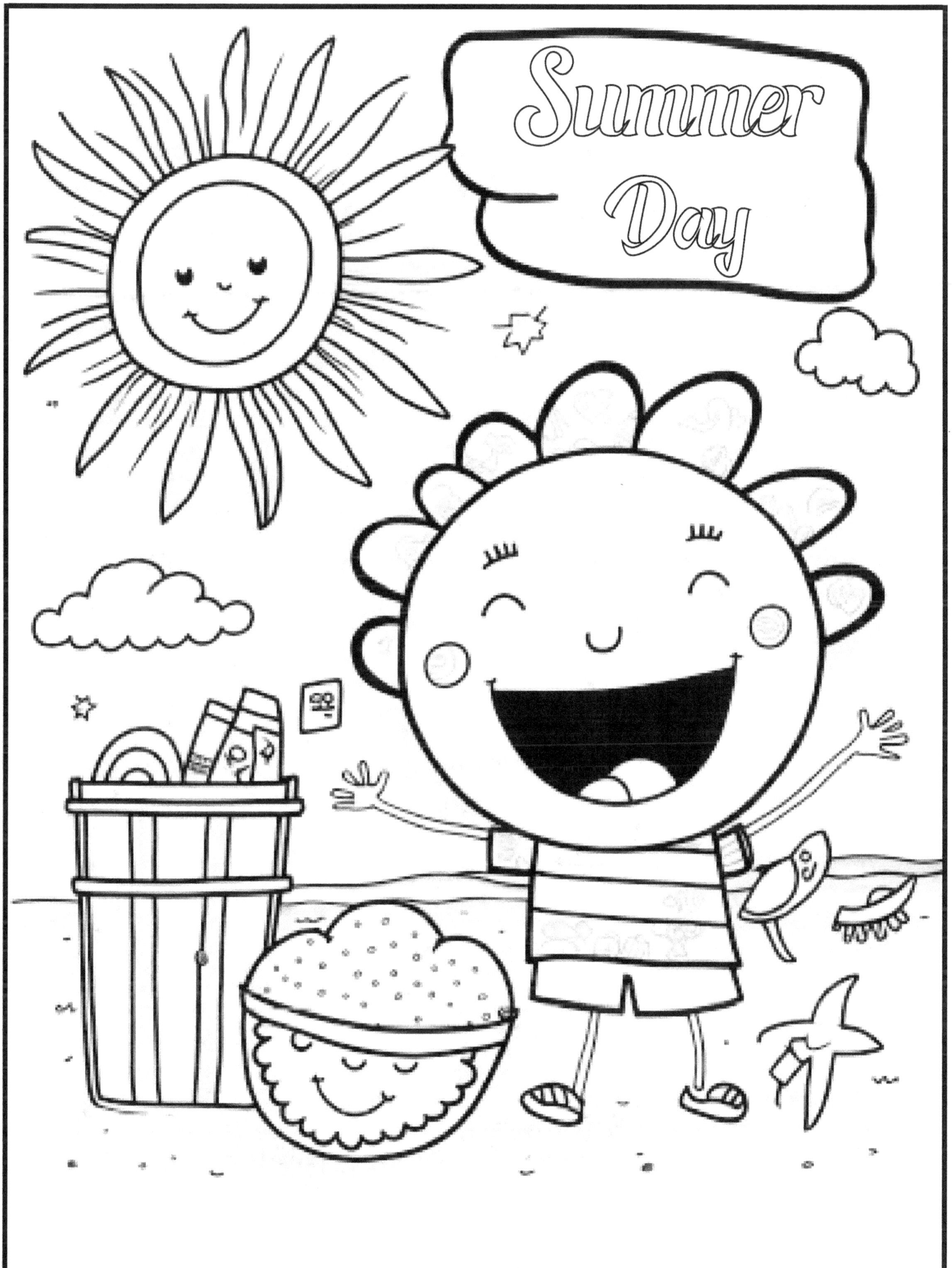
Summer Day

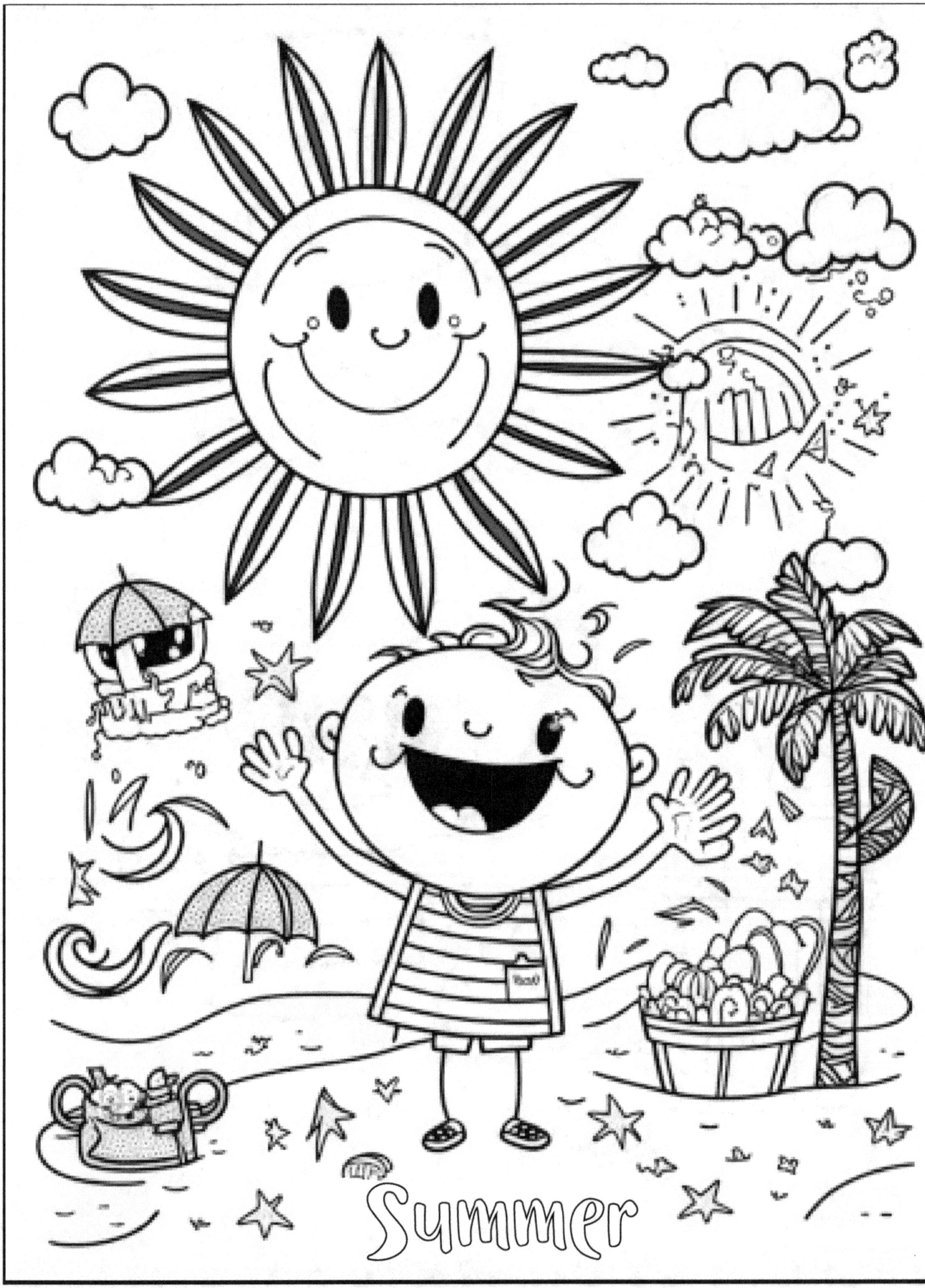
Summer

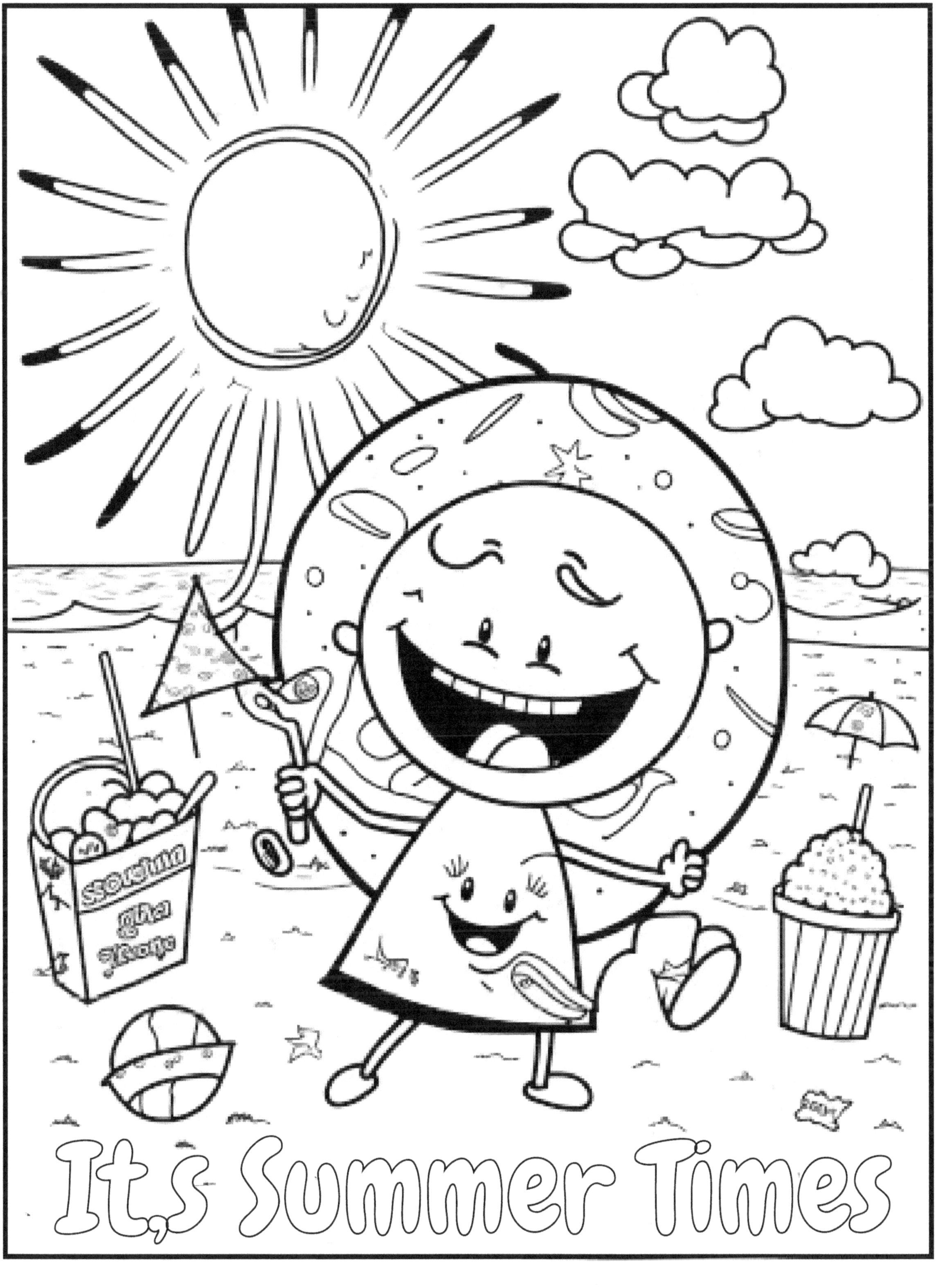
It,s Summer Times

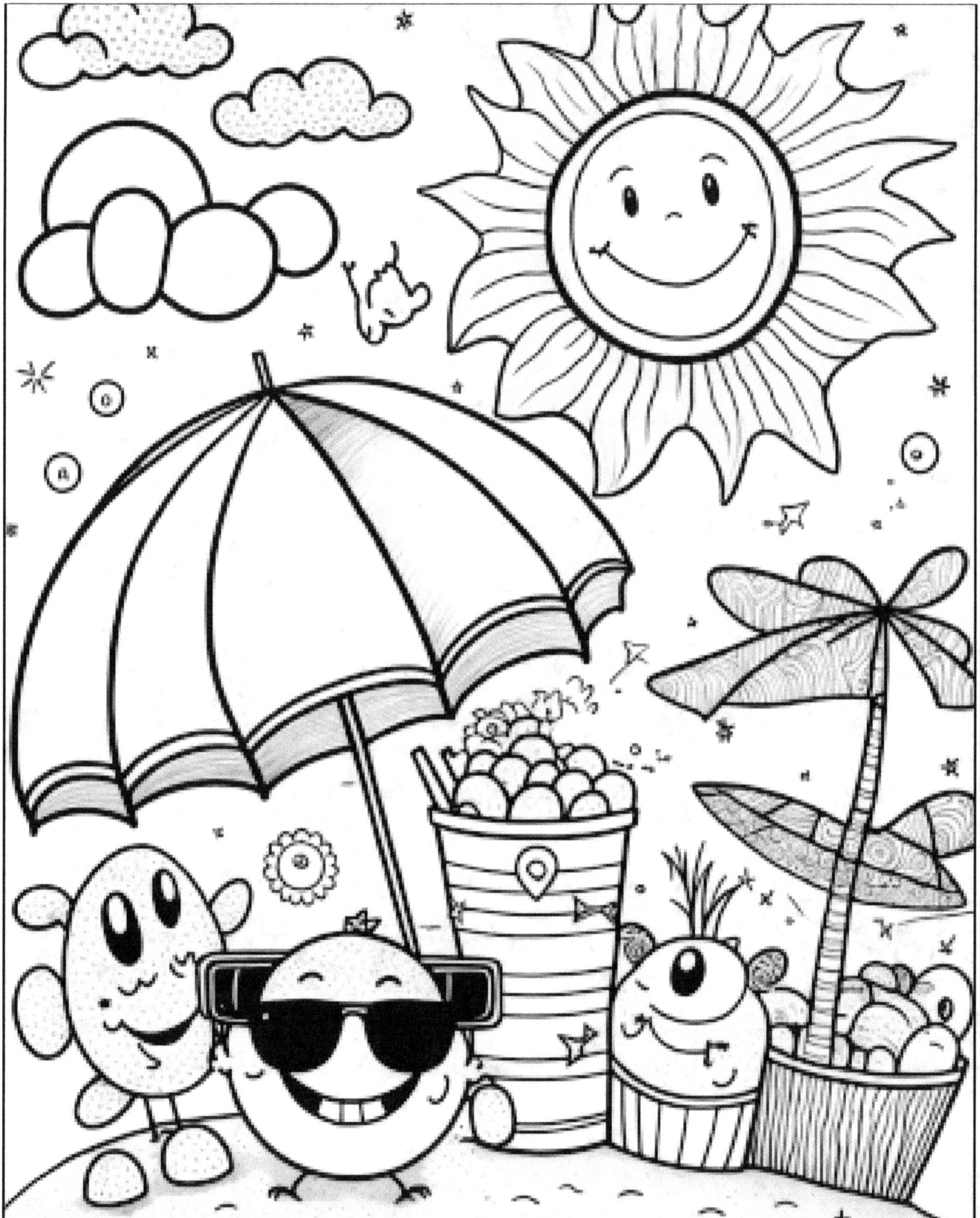
HAPPY SUMMER

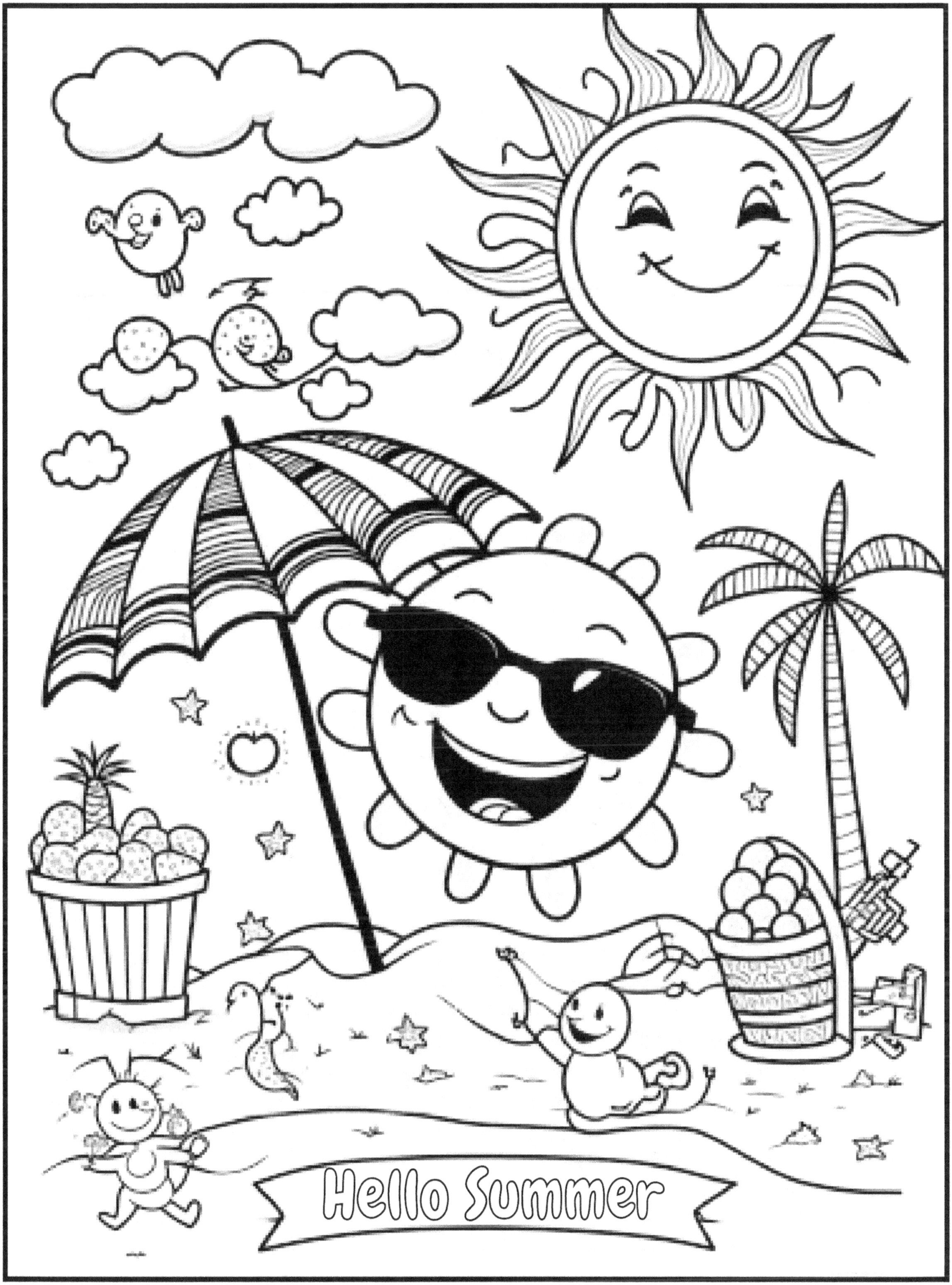
Hello Summer

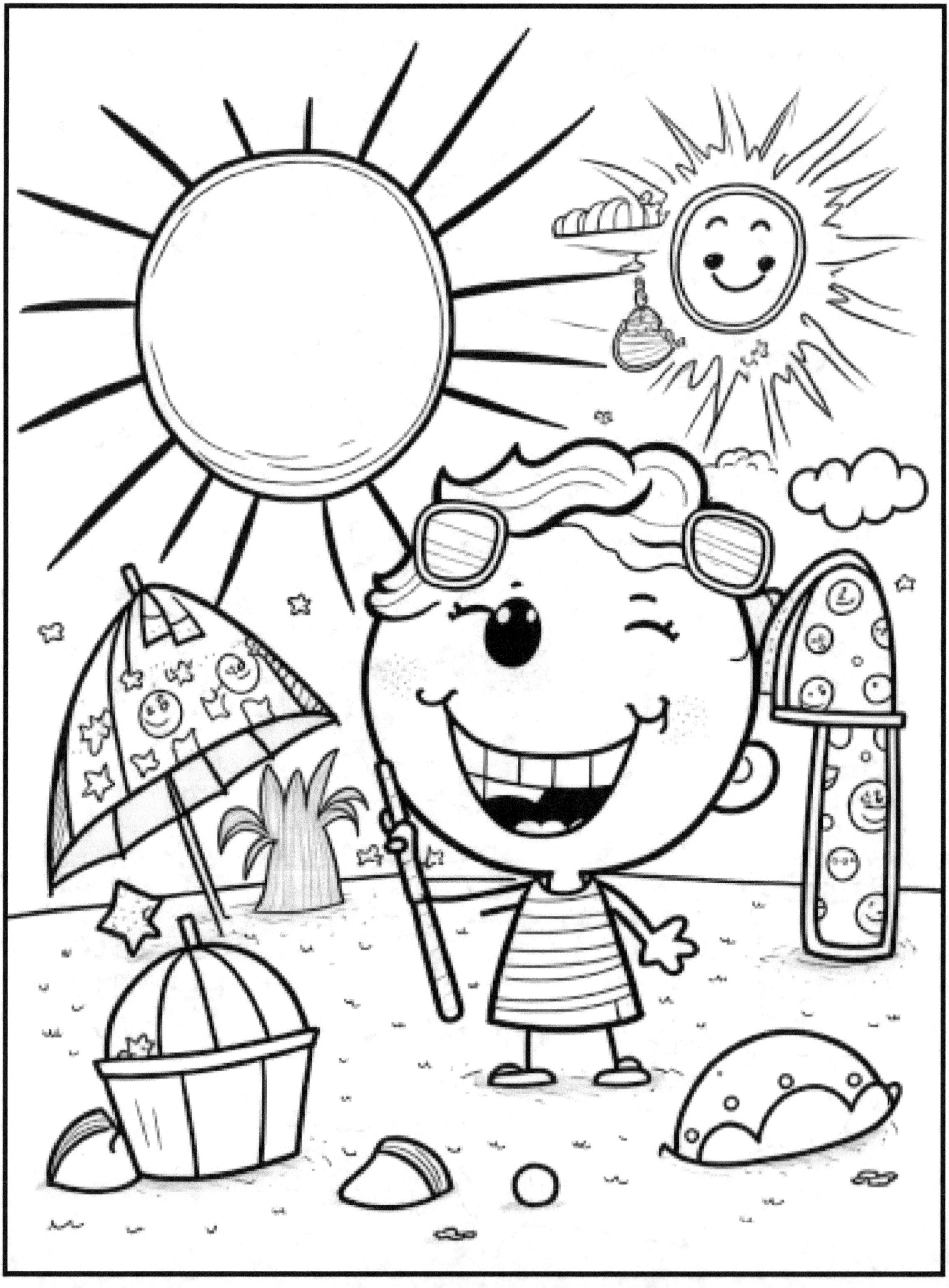

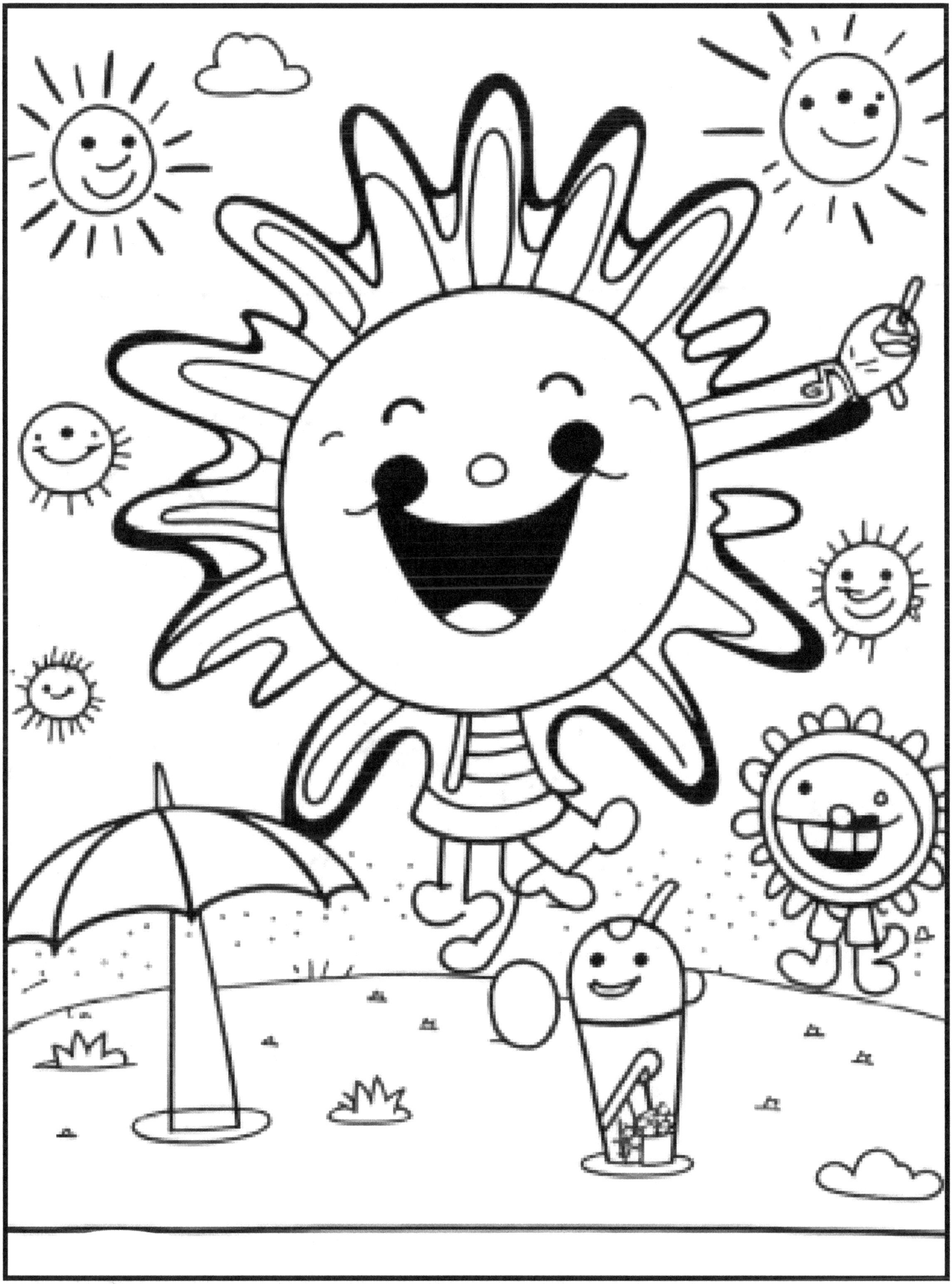

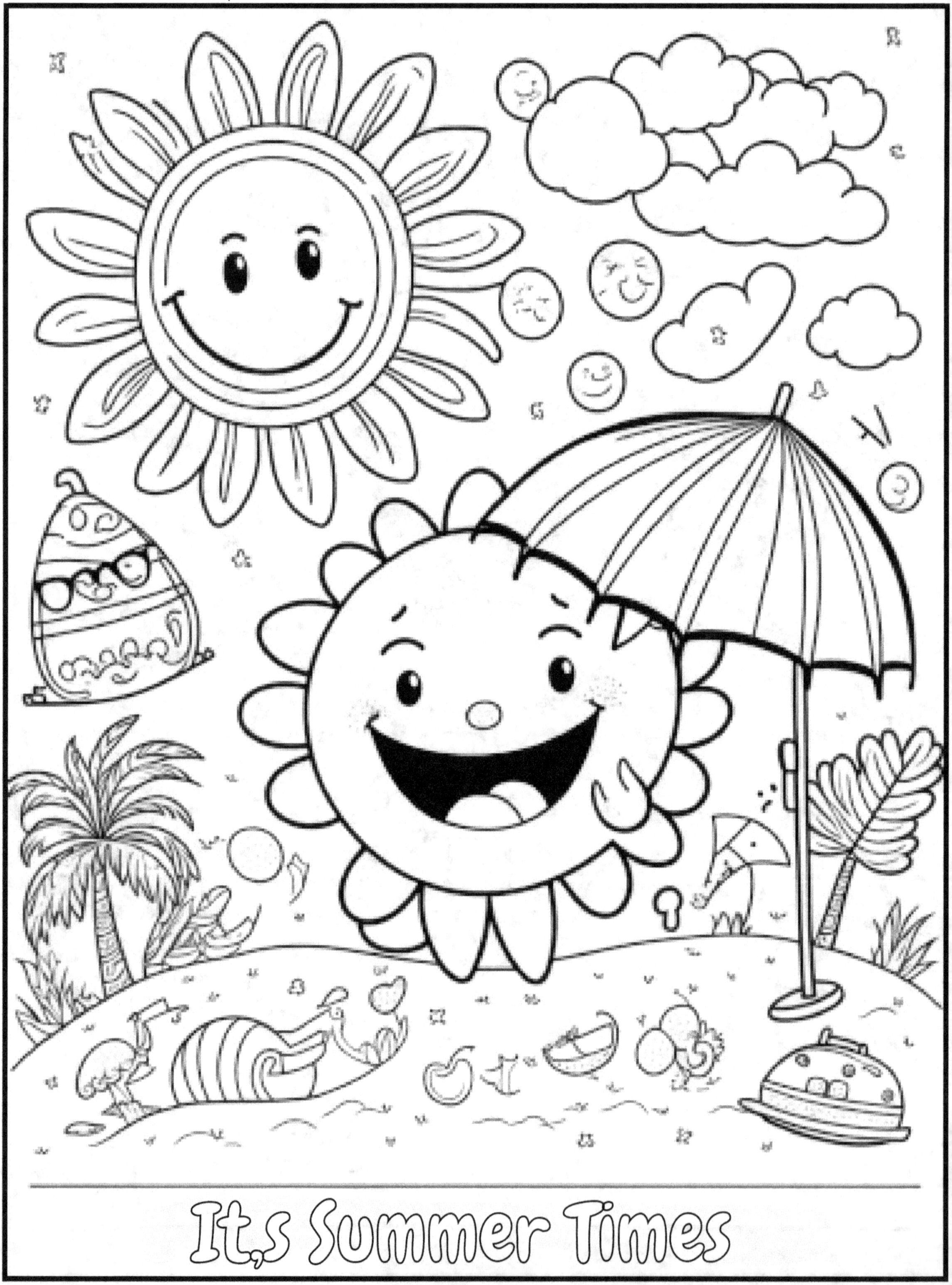

It,s Summer Times

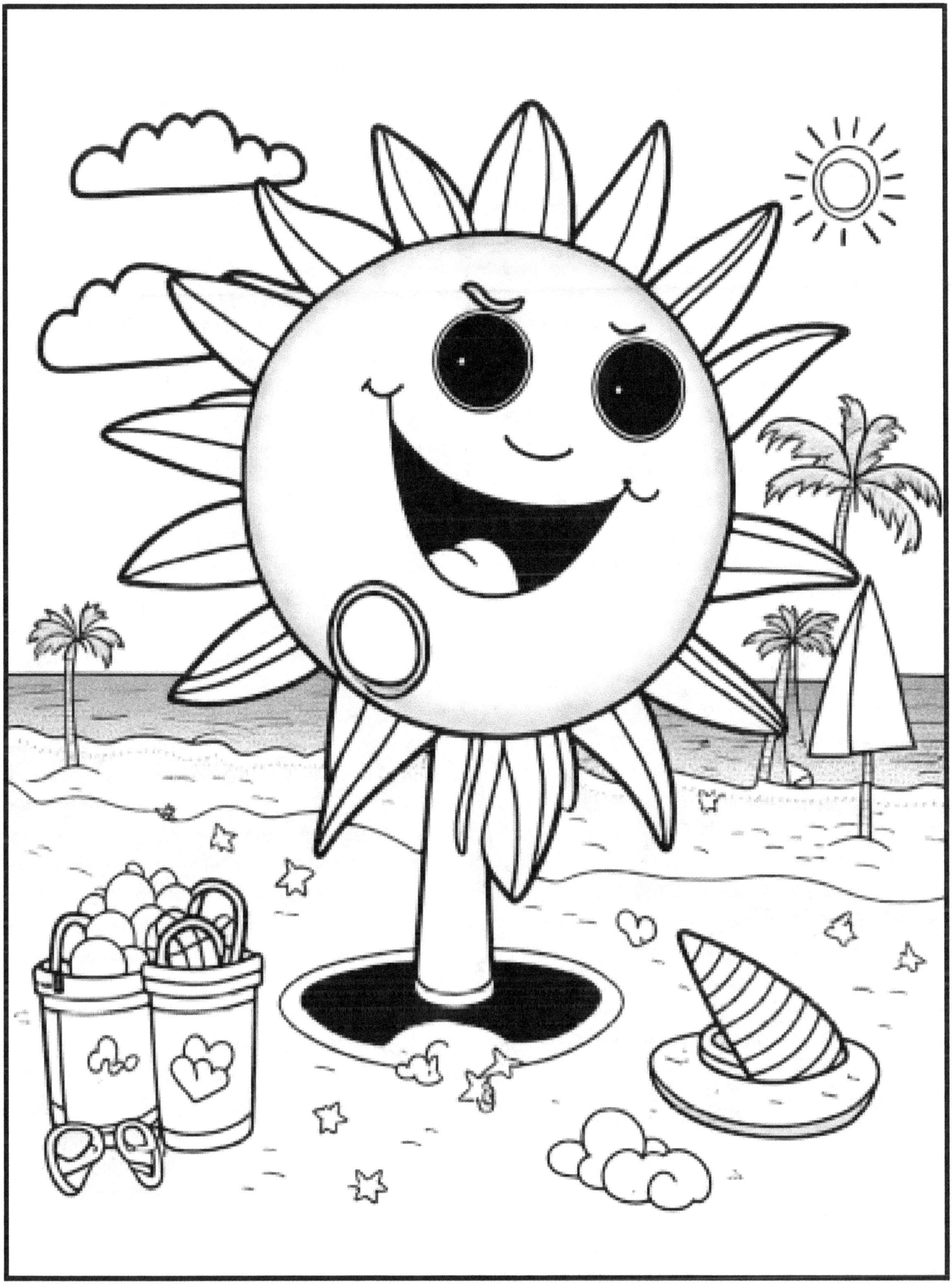

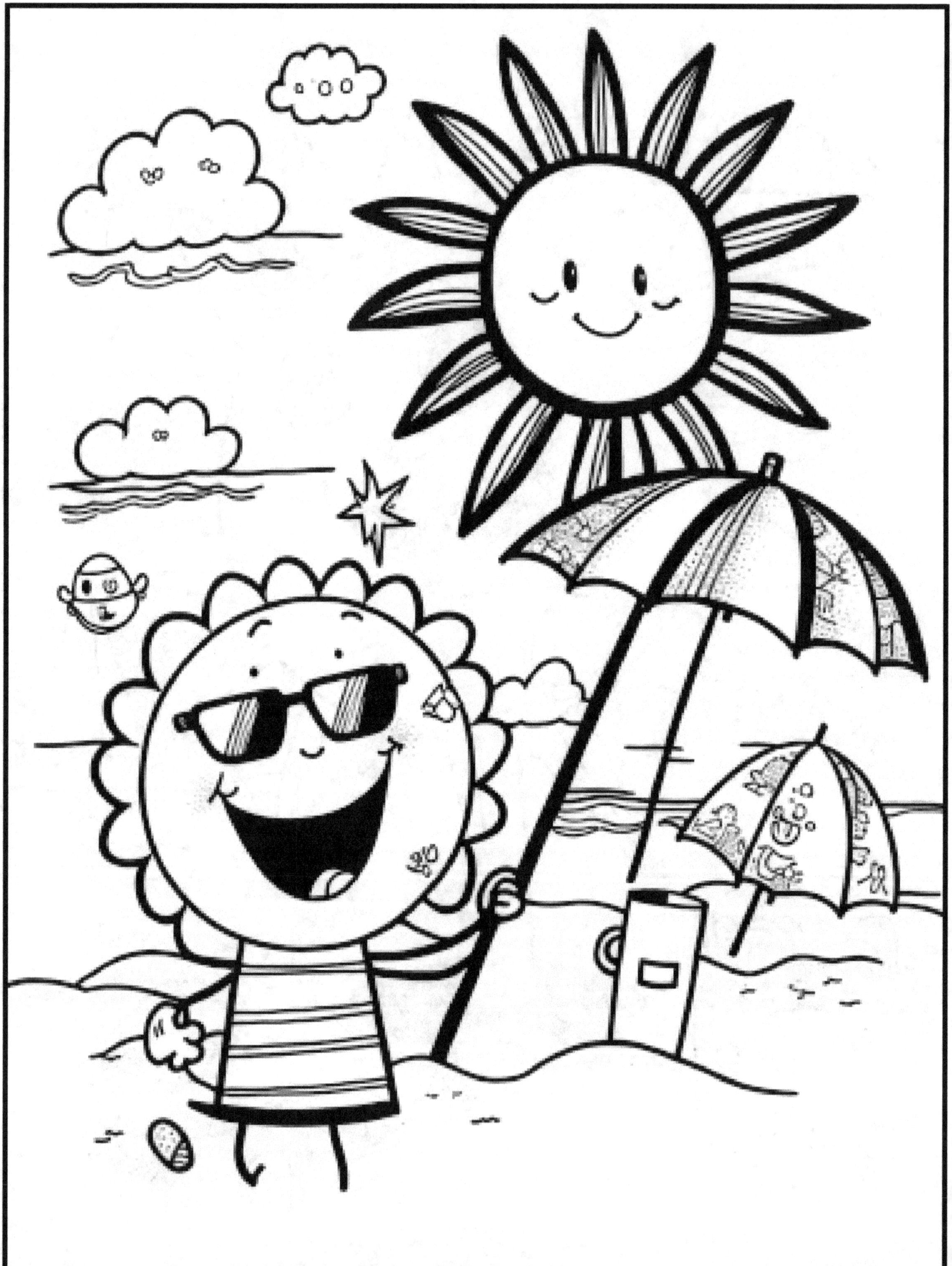

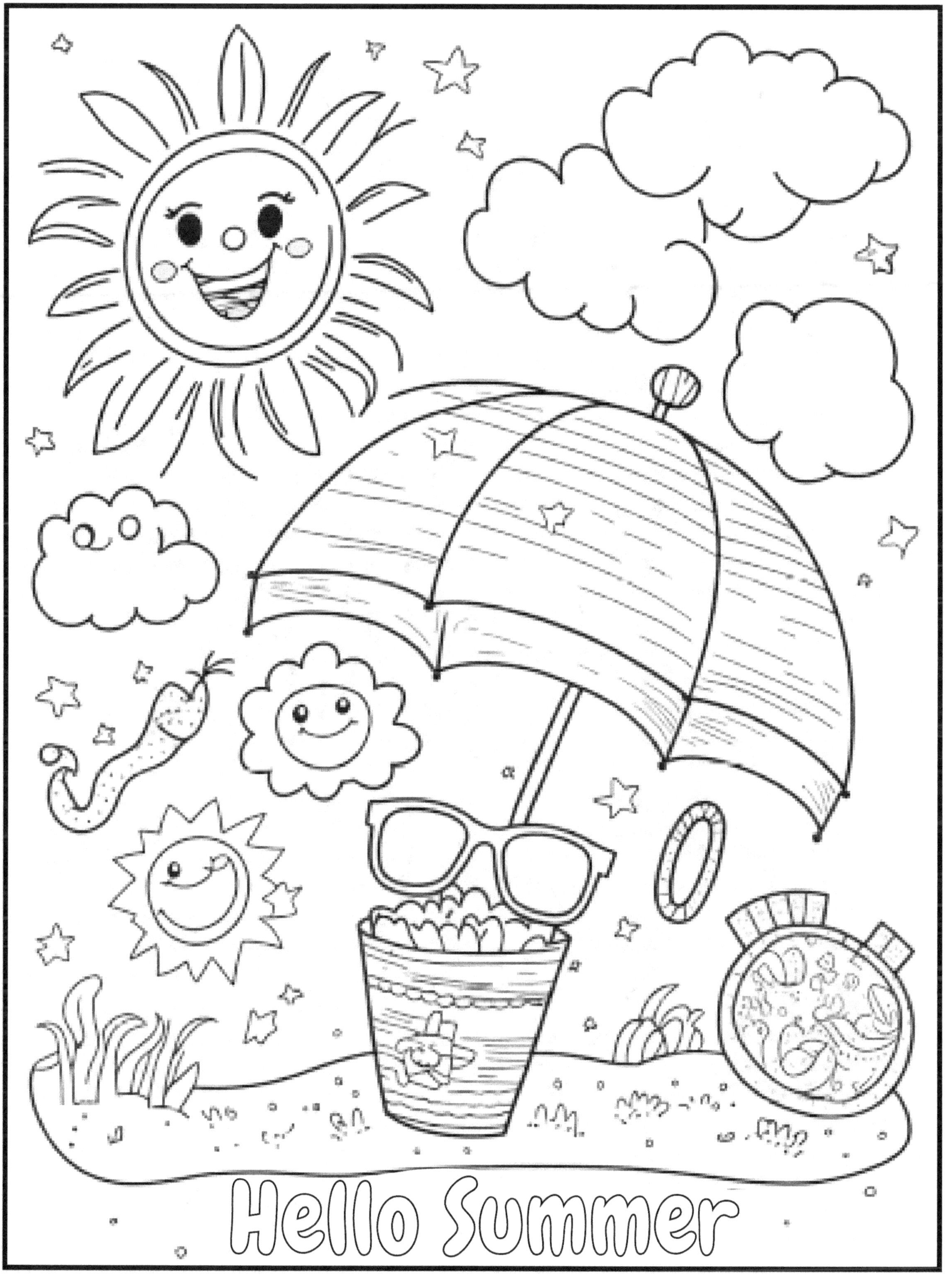
Hello Summer

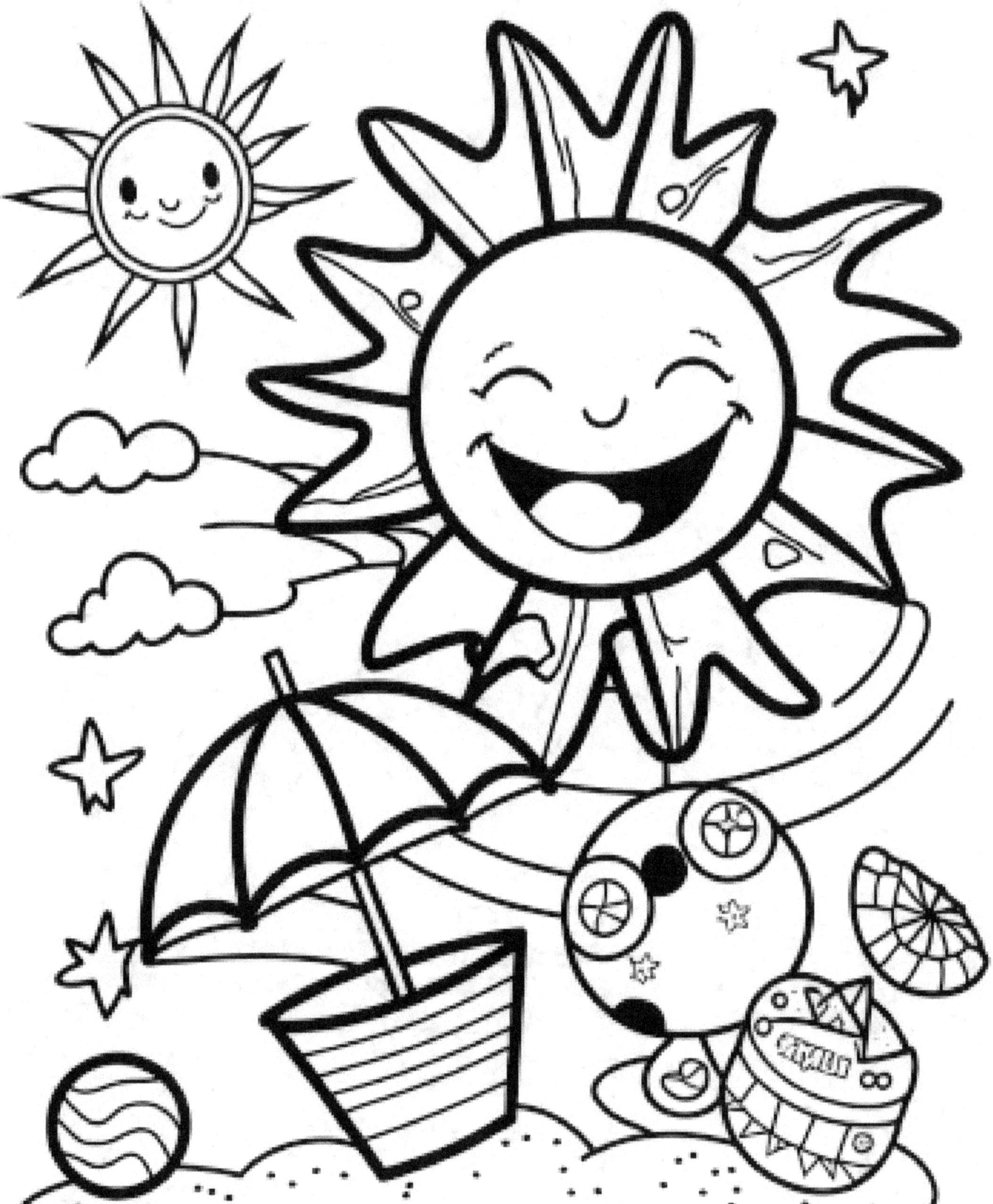

Summer Day

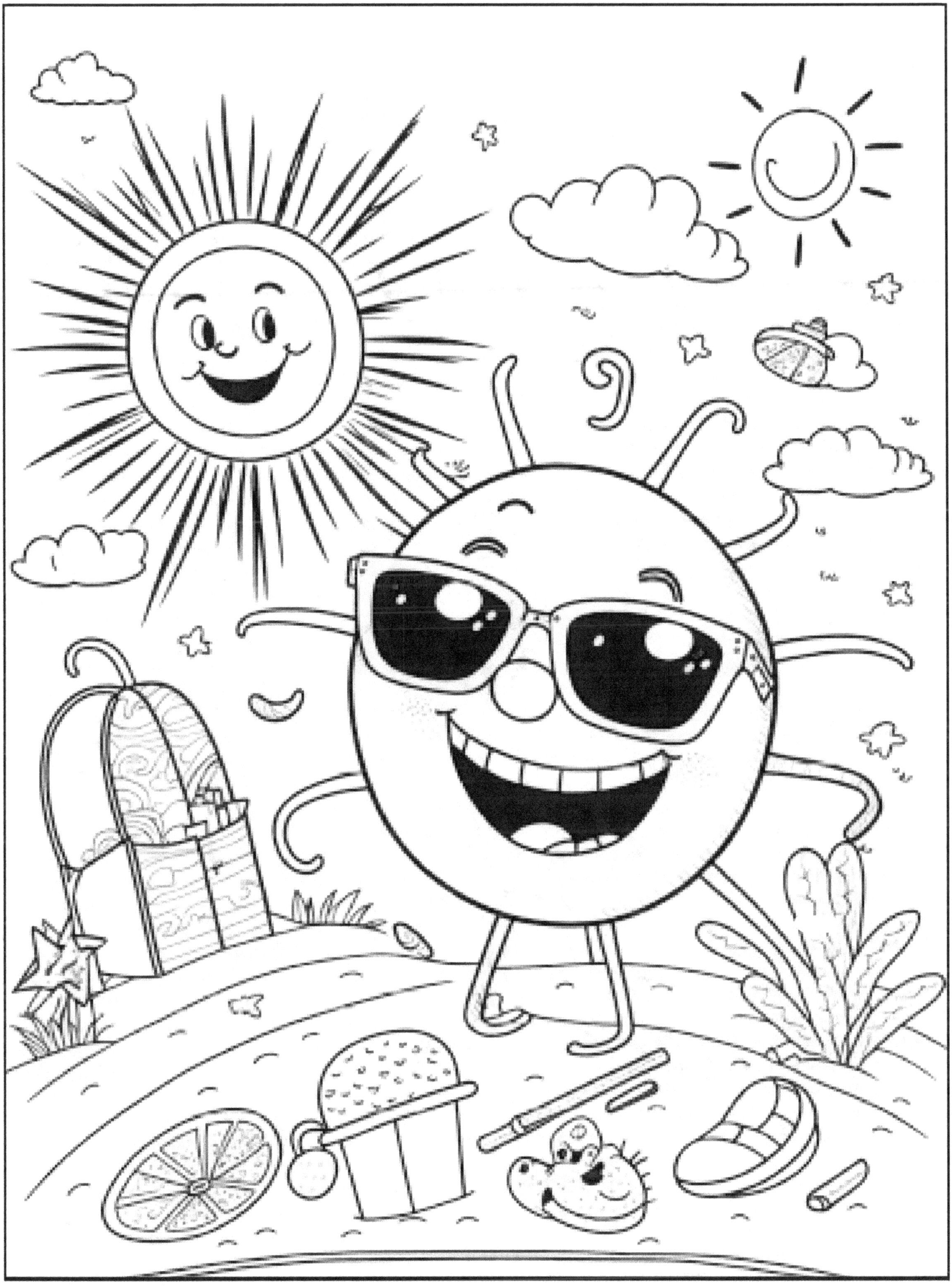

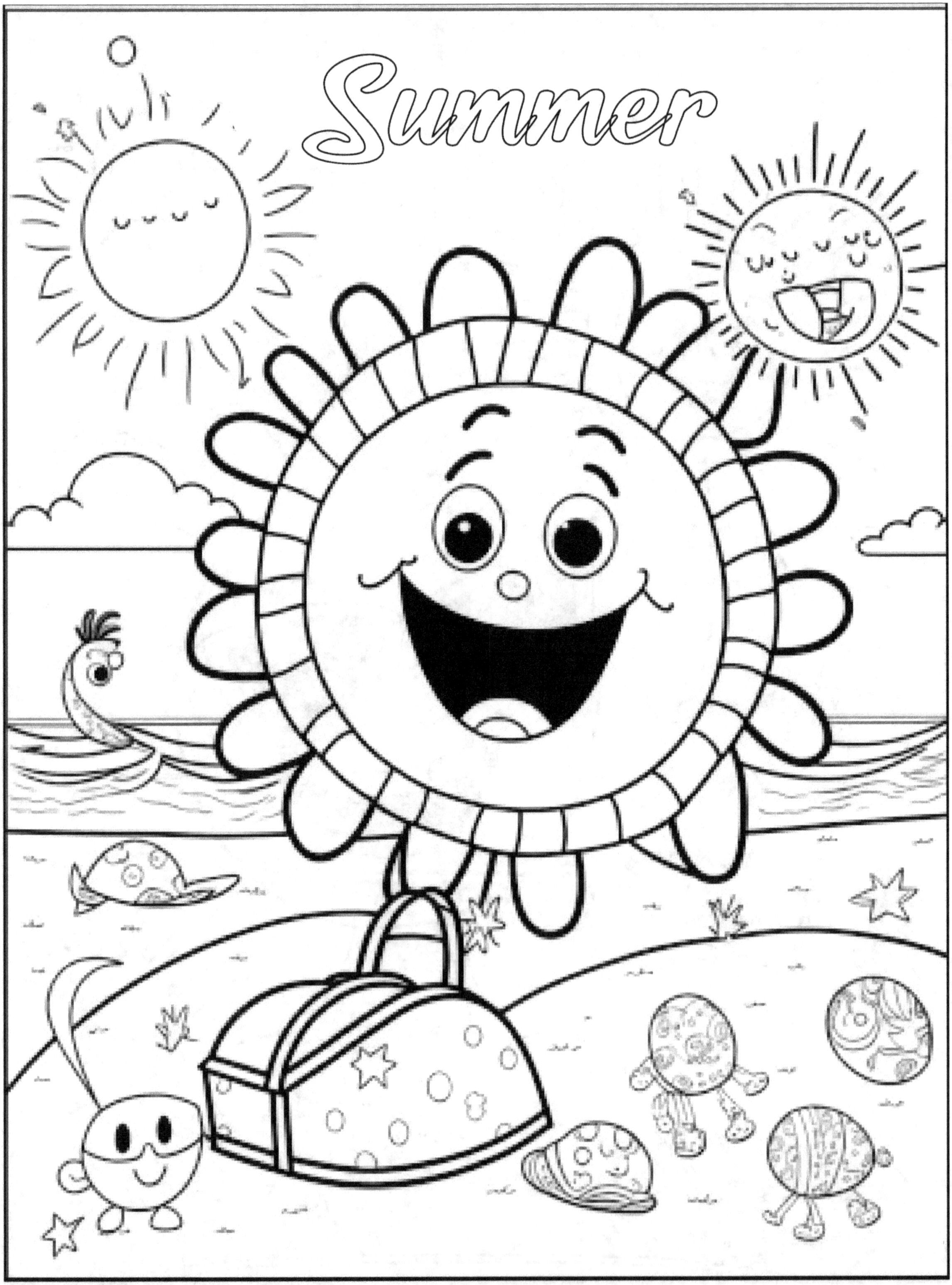
Summer

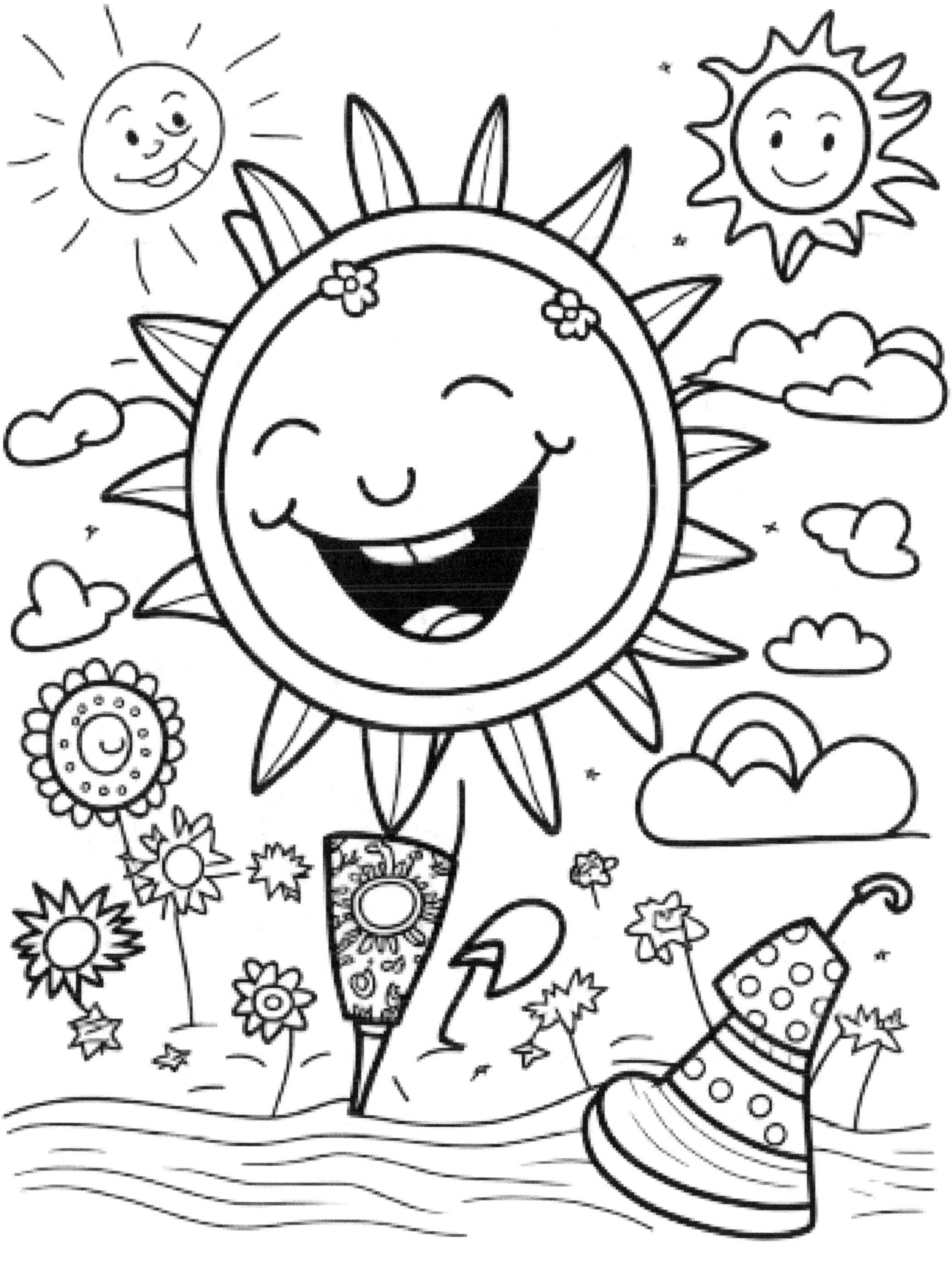

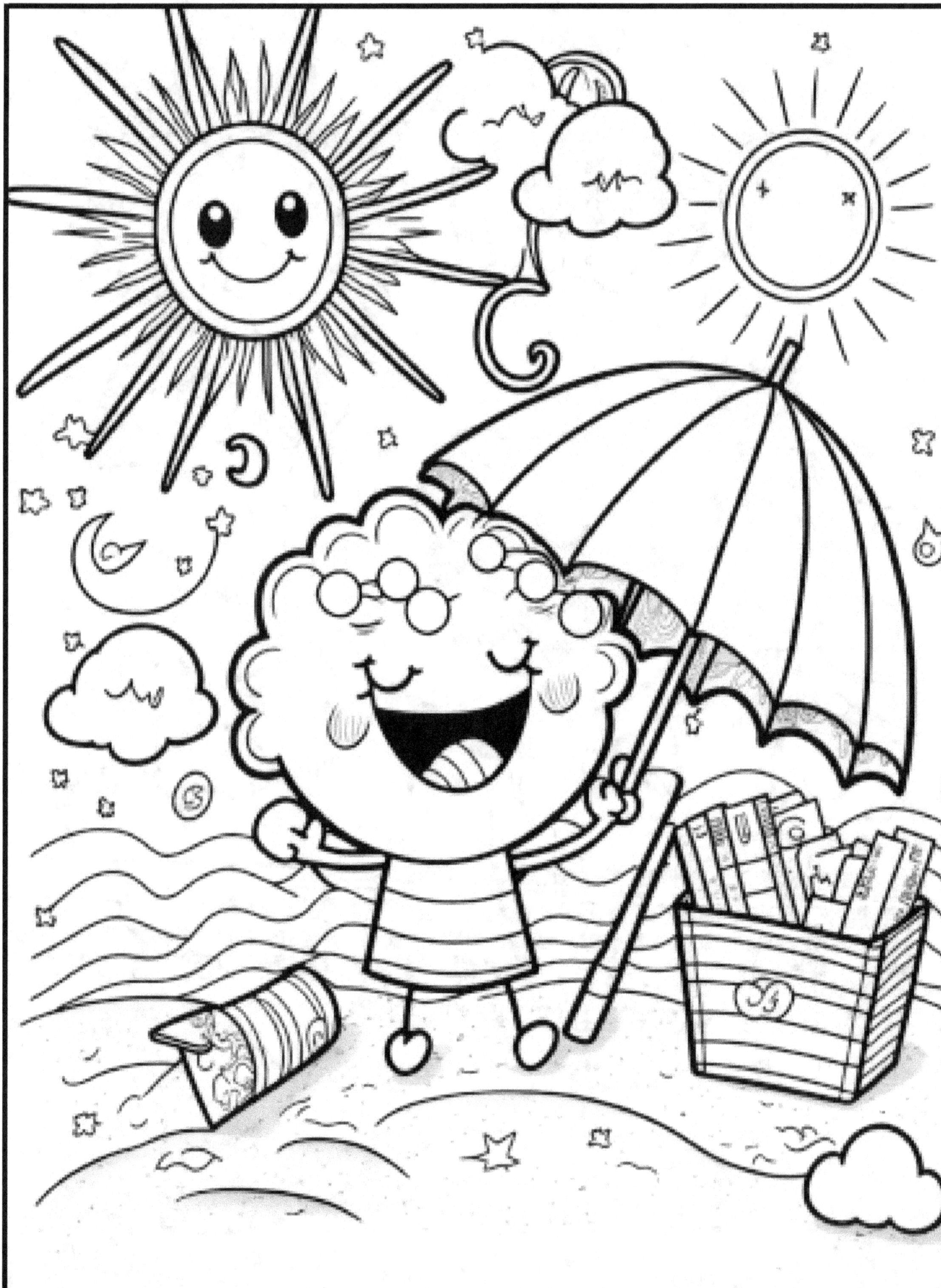

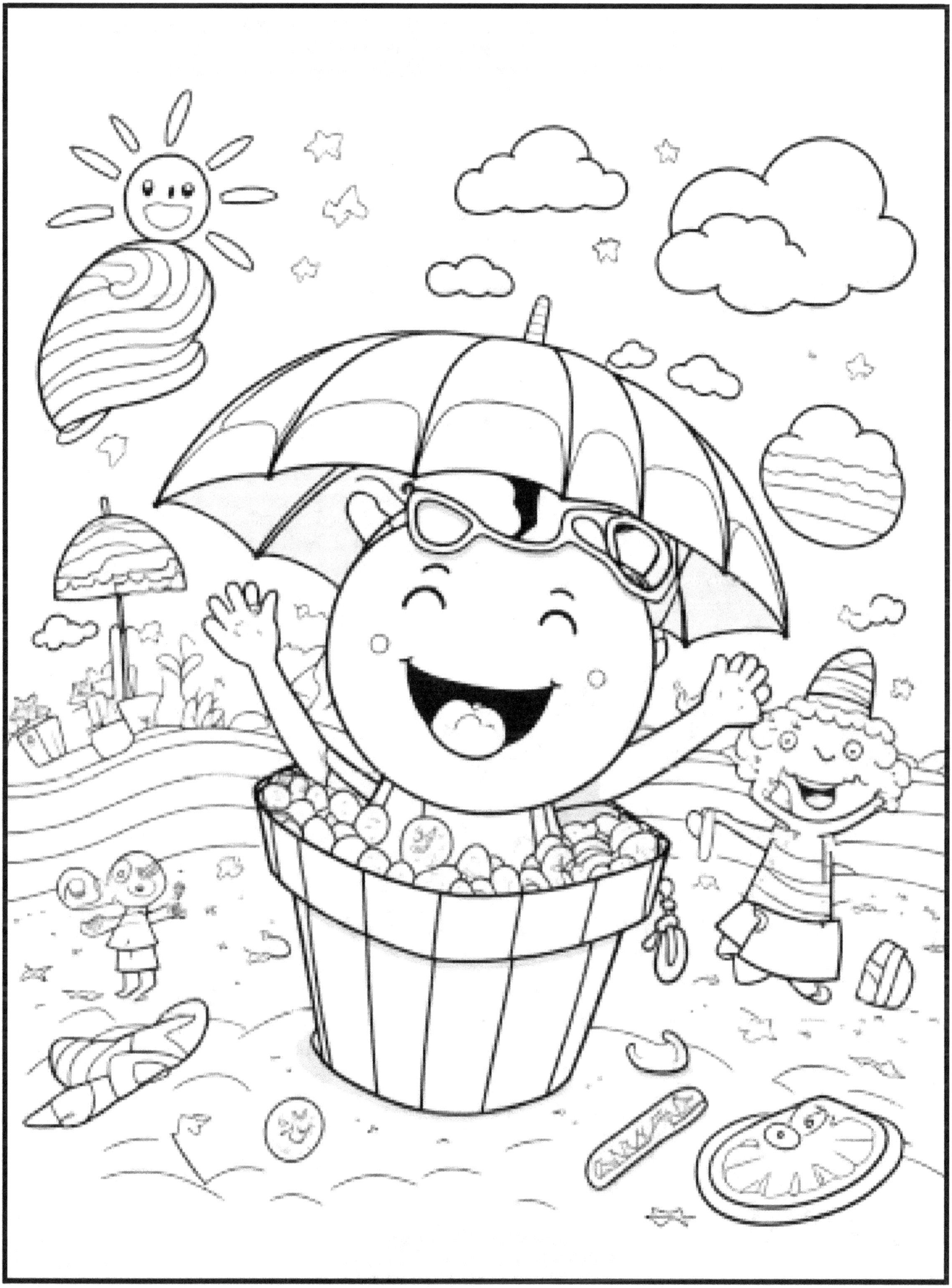

It,s Summer

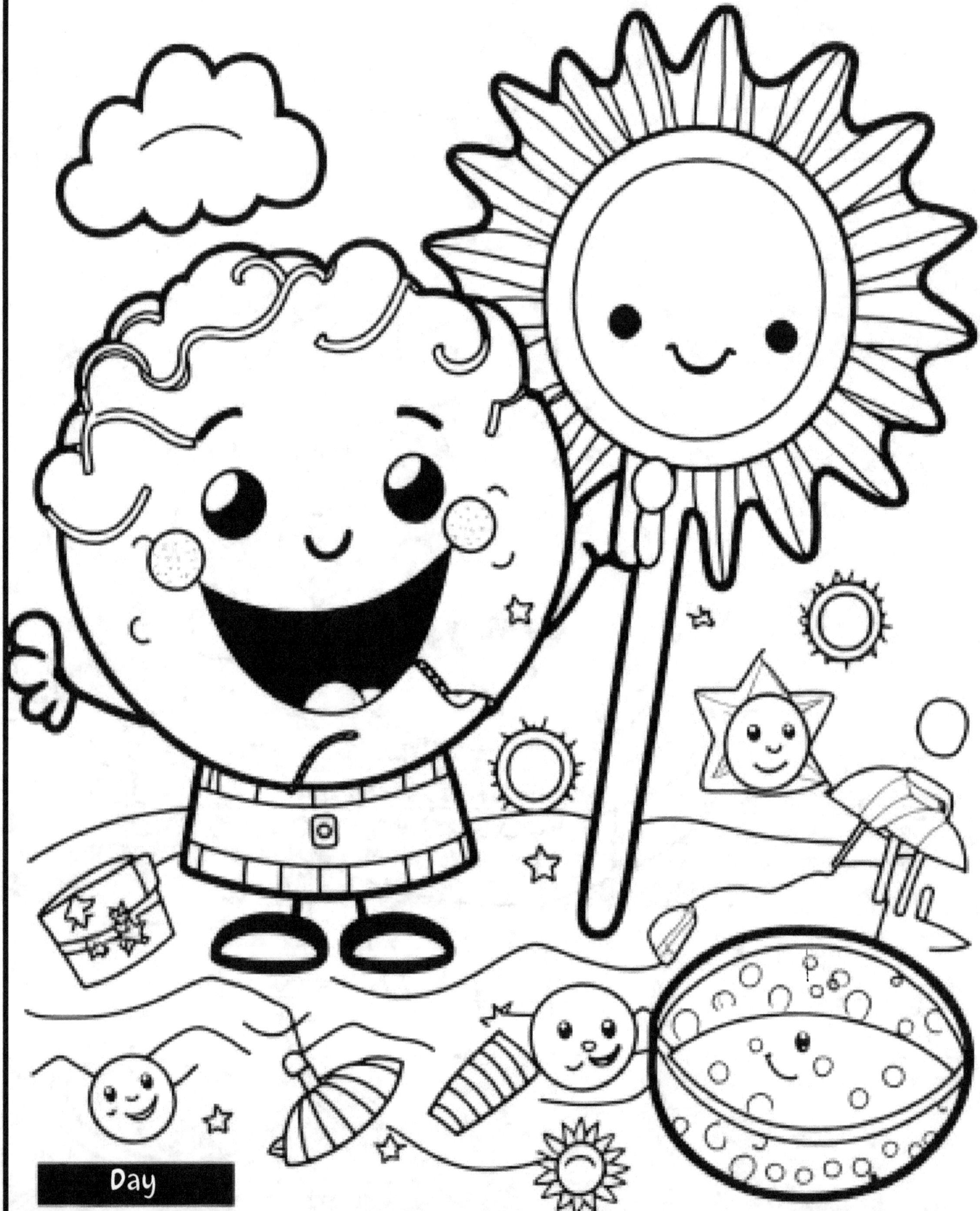

Day

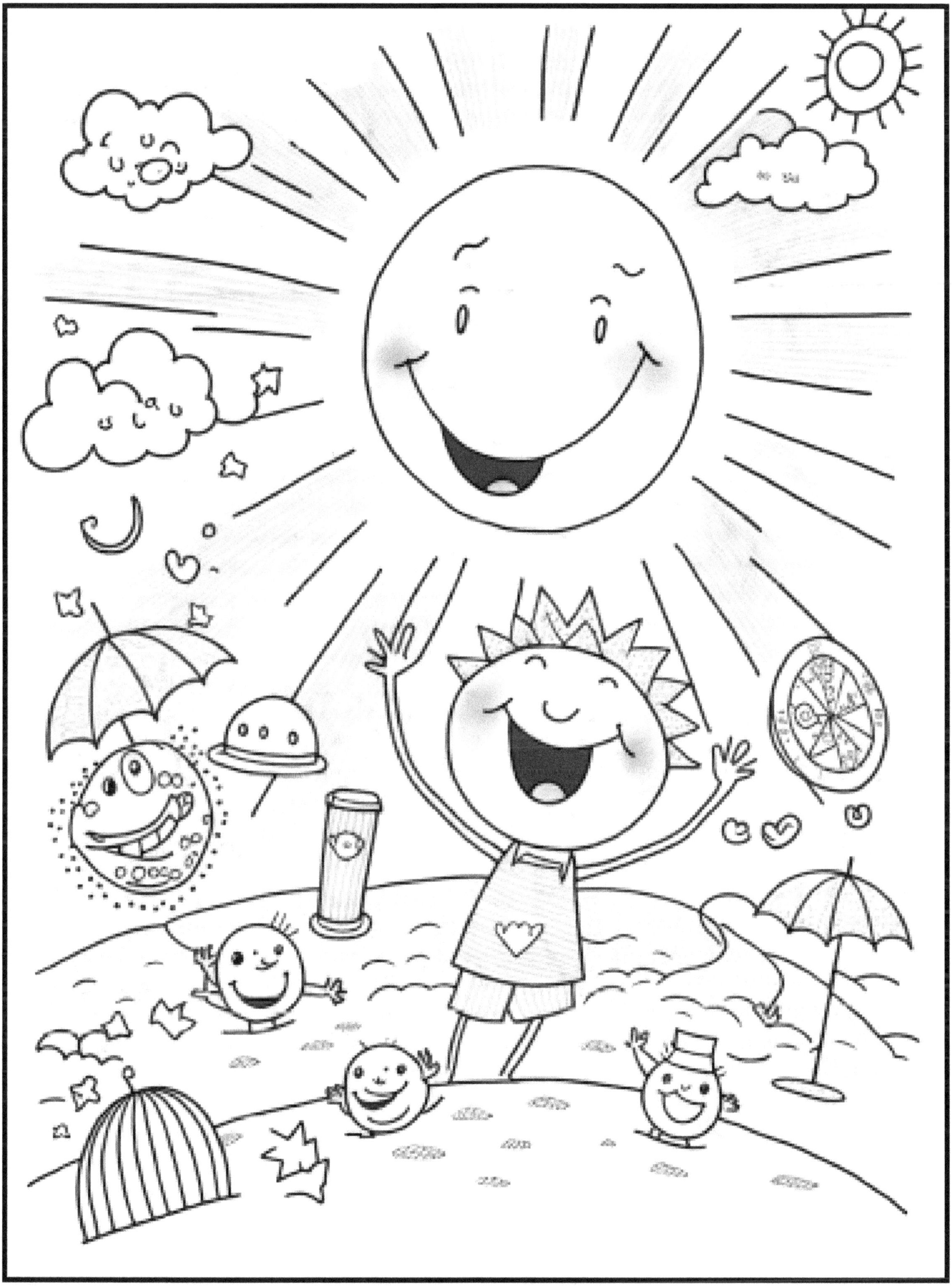

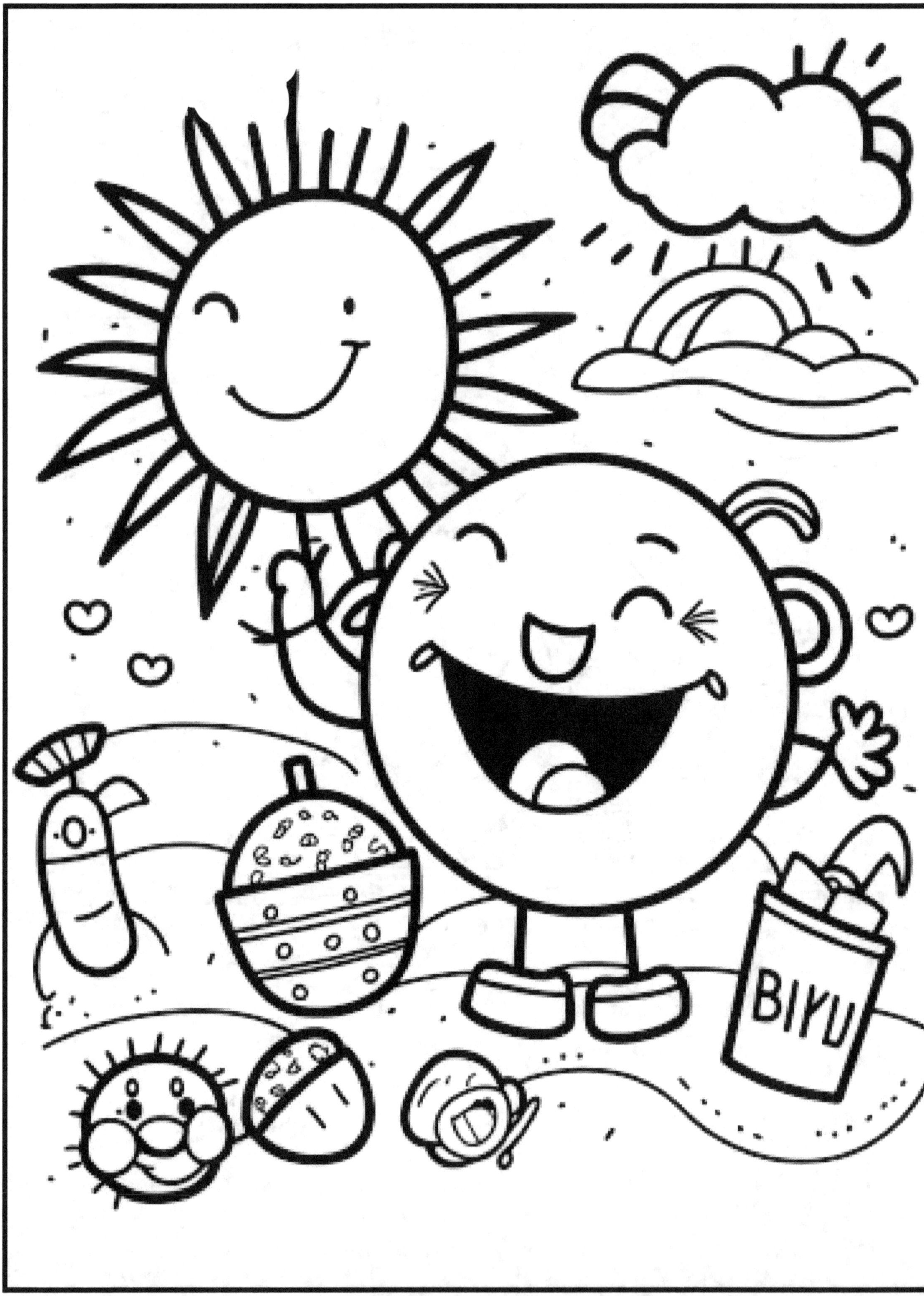
BIYU

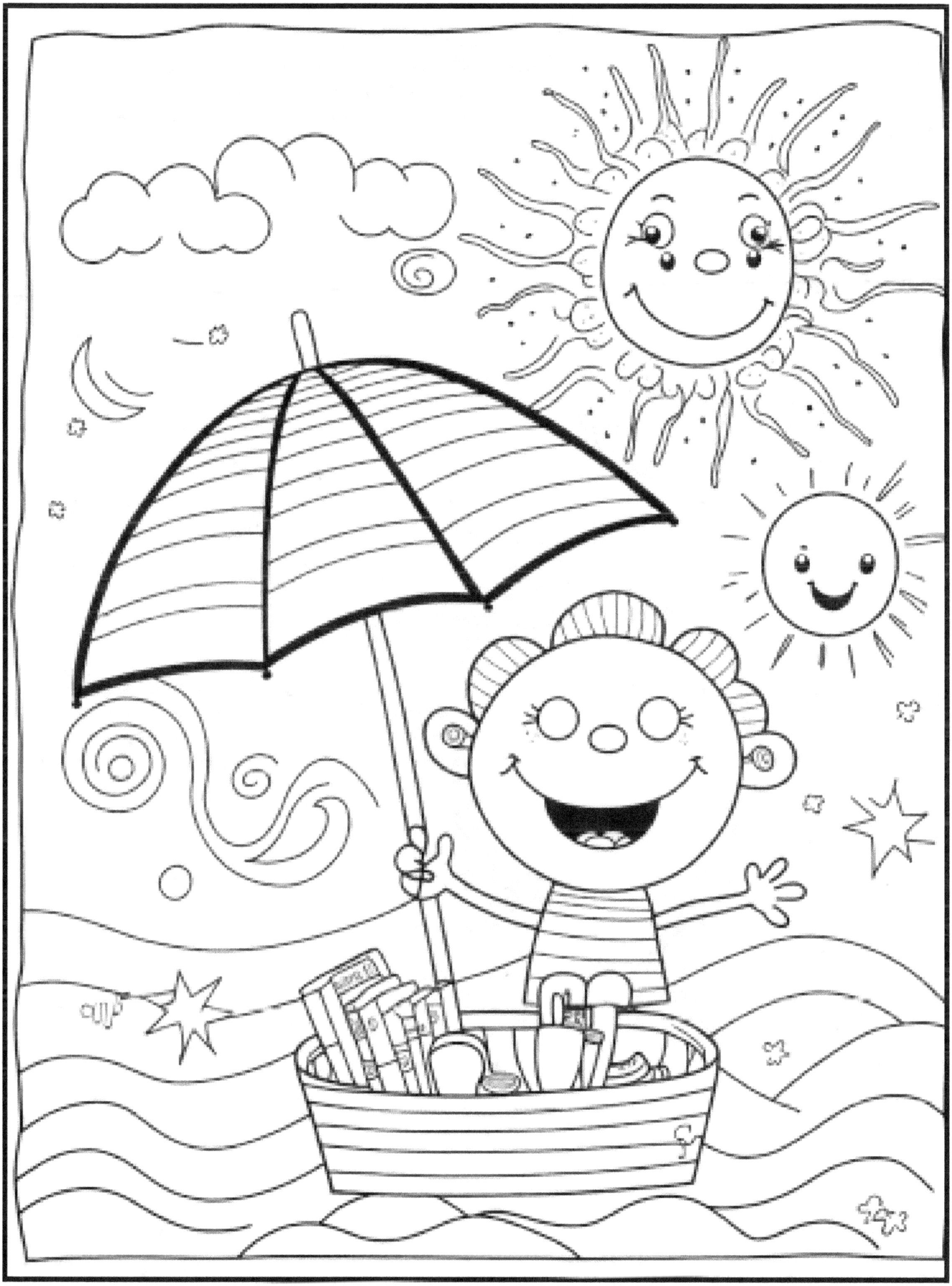

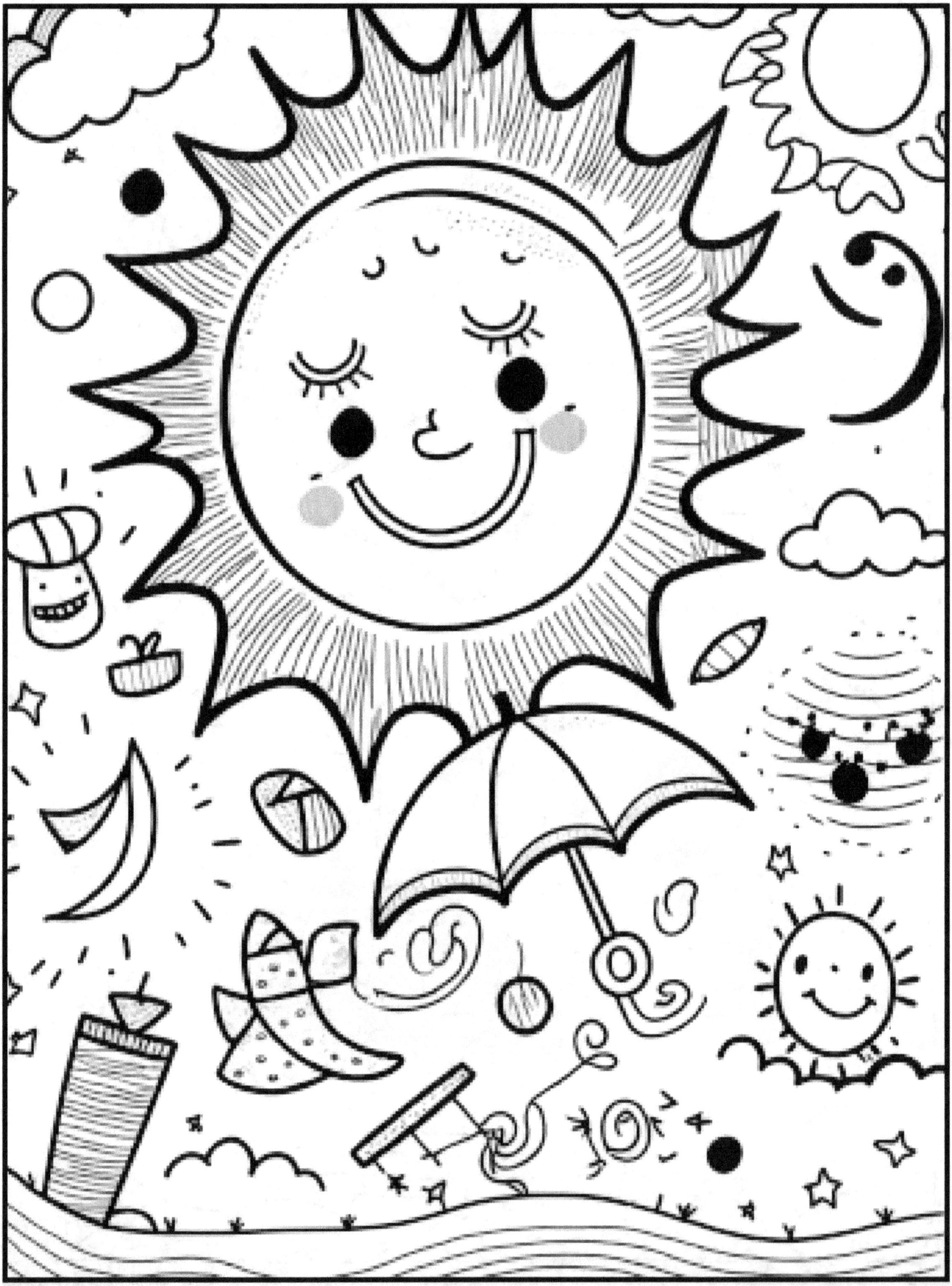

HAPPY SUMMER

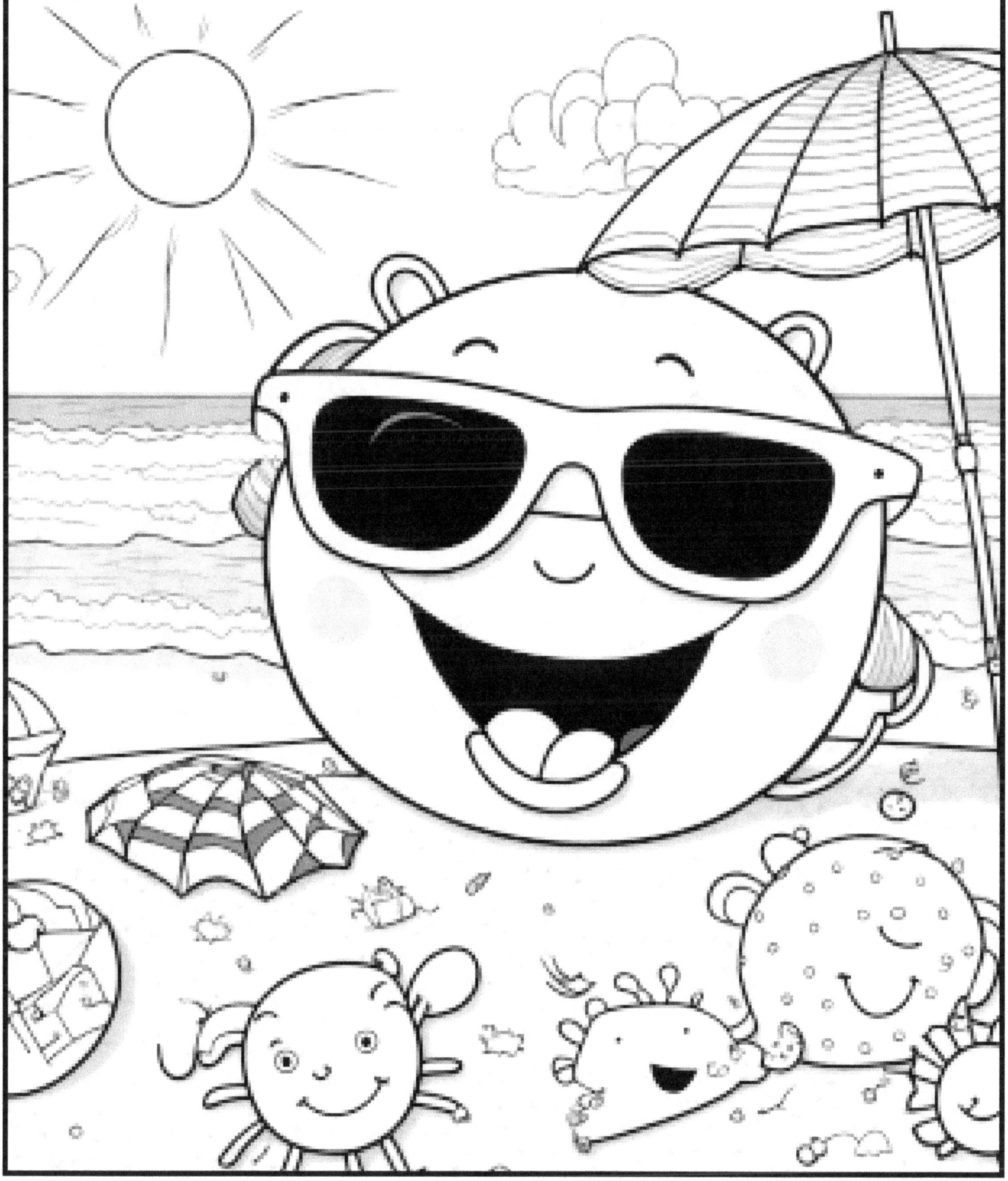

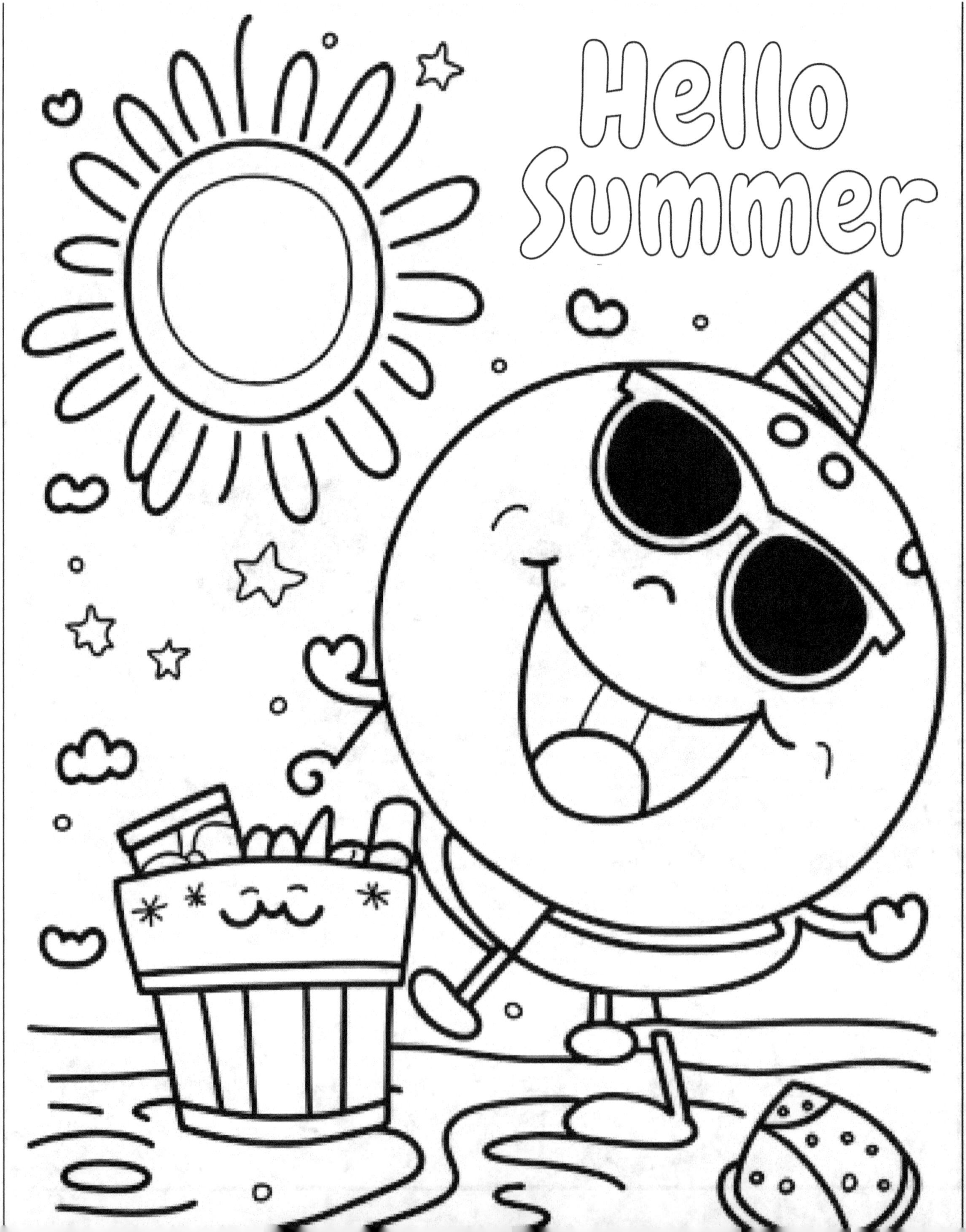
Hello
Summer

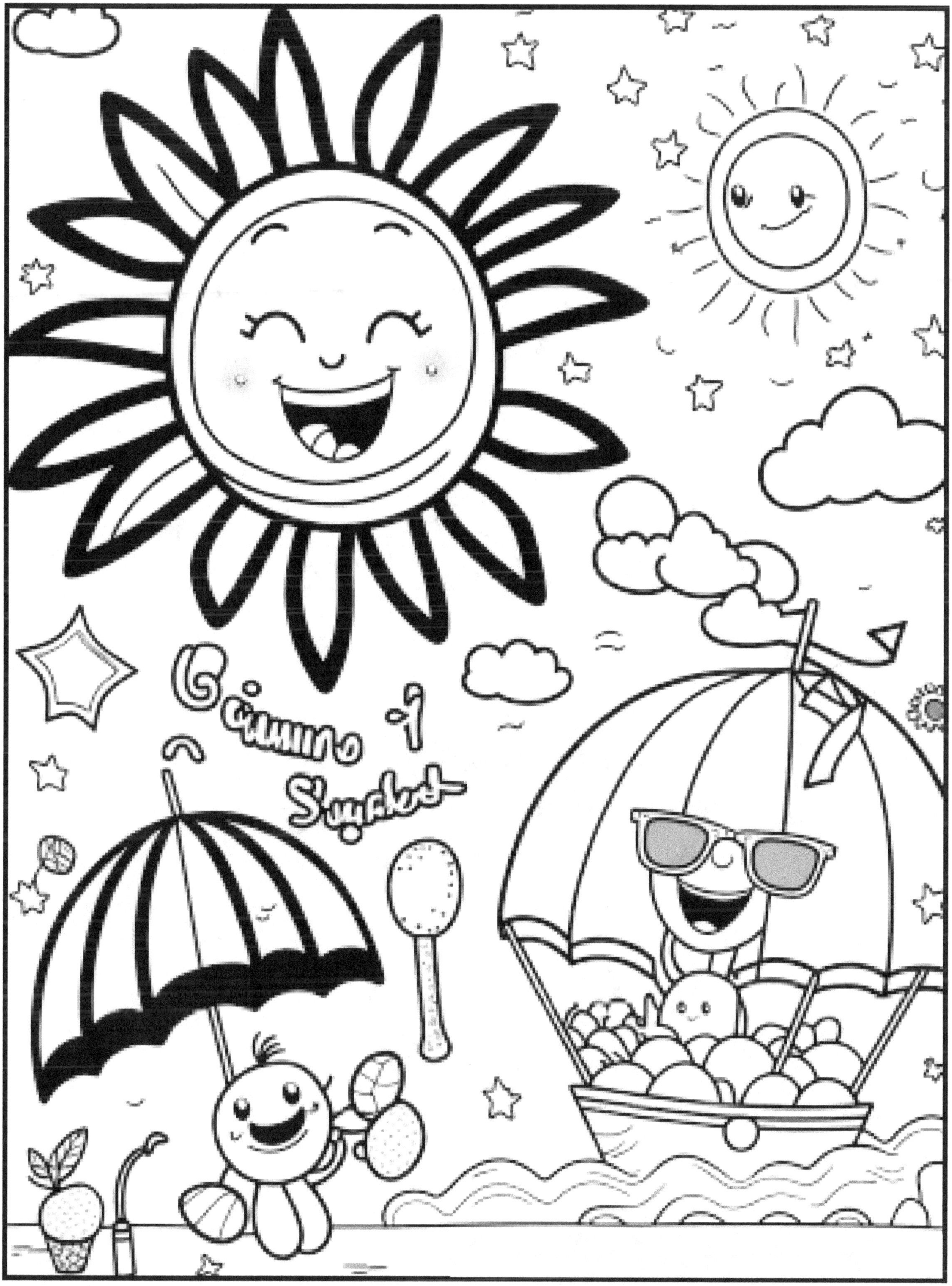

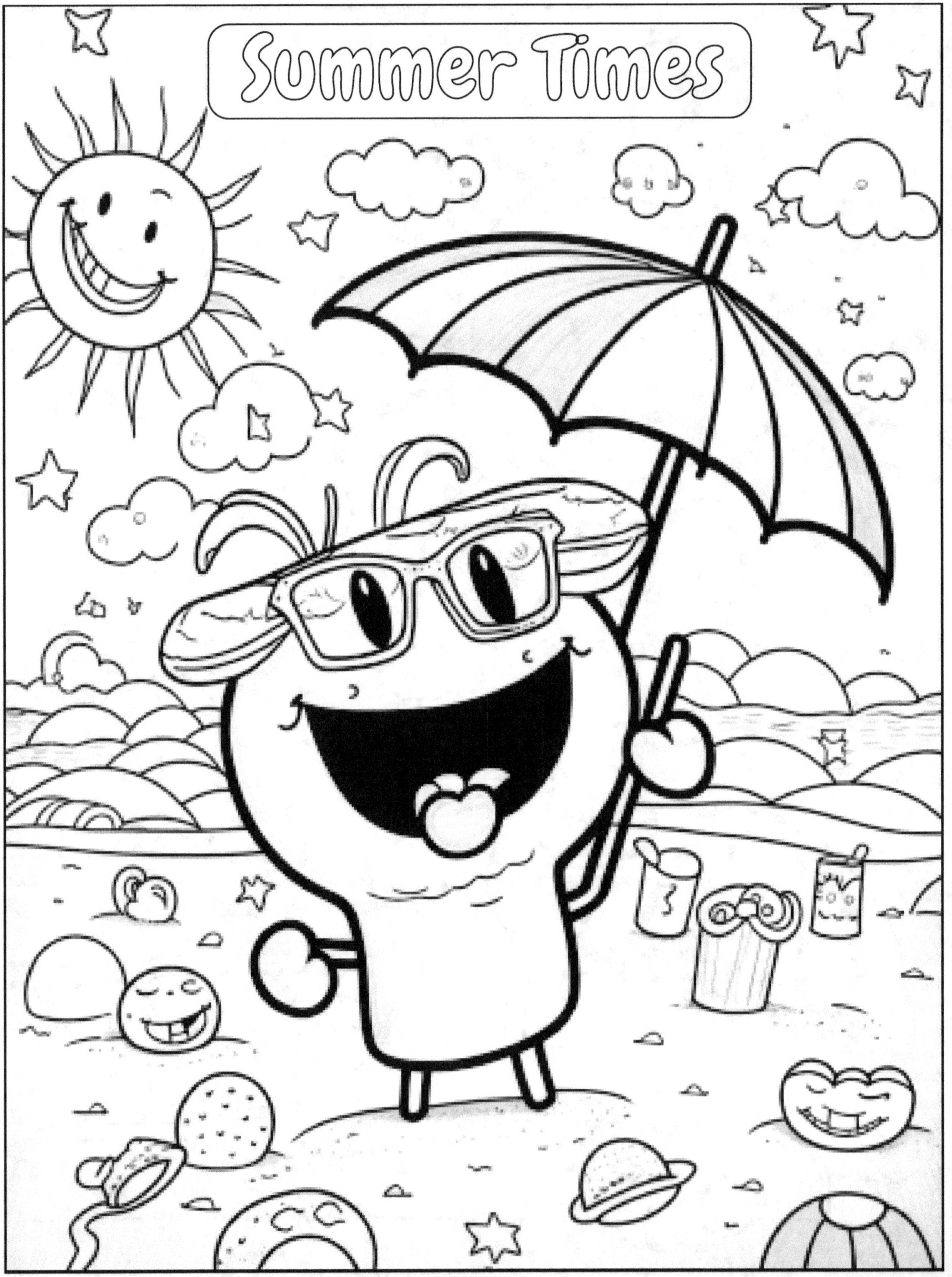
Summer Times

www.ingramcontent.com/pod-product-compliance
Lightning Source LLC
Chambersburg PA
CBHW081705220526
45466CB00009B/2885
* 9 7 9 8 3 9 7 6 6 0 5 2 5 *